God, the Christian, and Human Suffering

Herwig Arts, S.J.

Translated by Helen Rolfson, O.S.F.

1 18 27 4

A Liturgical Press Book

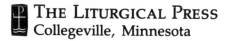 THE LITURGICAL PRESS
Collegeville, Minnesota

This book is translated from *Waarom Moeten Mensen Lijden?* published by Davidsfonds, Leuven, Belgium, 1985.

Cover design by Ann Blattner
Illustration by Ethel Boyle

1   2   3   4   5   6   7   8   9

Library of Congress Cataloging-in-Publication Data

Arts, Herwig.
    [Waarom moeten mensen lijden? English]
    God, the Christian, and human suffering / Herwig Arts ; translated by Helen Rolfson.
        p.   cm.
    Translation of: Waarom moeten mensen lijden?
    ISBN 0-8146-2100-7
    1. Suffering—Religious aspects—Christianity. 2. Theodicy.
I. Title
BT732.7.A7713   1993
231'.8—dc20   92-43239
                                                         CIP

*For Cathy and Marijke, and for the many who,
like Mary, became mothers of a suffering child.*

Contents

Introduction

How can a good and almighty God allow so much innocent suffering? Moreover, how can this same God remain
mute before the prayer of so many good people who beg
for healing, help, or deliverance? Is God incapable of
preventing that suffering? Is it not in God's power to
create a world without all that heaven-rending evil? If that
is the case, we can scarcely call God "almighty." But if
God really is almighty, then we have a hard time understanding God's non-intervention or refusal to intervene.
At first glance, it seems difficult to reconcile God's omnipotence with God's goodness.

When we look at the countless forms of suffering and
evil in the world, it begins to seem that the much-exalted
omnipotence and goodness of God are only very relative
concepts. If God can prevent evil, then why does God not
do it? And if God really cannot prevent evil, why do we
pray in our need to a God who is "almighty"? These are
questions that have occupied the human race for centuries,
questions for which there is no immediate answer, not
even in the Bible; questions that sooner or later urge us all
to reflect on our own suffering and especially on the
suffering of those close to our hearts; questions nevertheless to which the Bible and a number of saints, mystics,
and the devout in the course of history have found an initial preamble to an answer. Inspired by them, we therefore
venture, in spite of everything, to write this book.

Unbelievers do not know what to do with this sort of
question. Therefore they discreetly relegate it to the do-
main of psychology. According to them, people must learn
to live with such insoluble questions and in the meantime

try to concentrate on less depressing subjects as much as they can.

But we cannot avoid the question about the real meaning and sense of suffering and evil. The answer we give (or do not give) for ourselves delimits the depth and the richness of our lives. Our judgment about suffering and death is the touchstone of our belief.

In our attempt to formulate a few meaningful reflections on the role of the negative element in this world, we take our stance as believing Christians. We do this, not out of random option or purely personal preference, but with the firm conviction that with respect to suffering there are only three conceivable attitudes: faith, pure psychology, or hopeless silence. To us, the second stance seems too superficial and the third defeatist.

First, we shall reflect on the formulation of the problem itself. Are the questions correctly framed? Next, we will look for an answer that is more than an abstract theory or a pious phrase. Therefore, we will consult representatives of those within the rich Christian tradition, as well as those from without. Moreover, we will ask if each of us, from our own personal (more or less limited) experience of suffering, has not caught a glimpse of some light which makes the witness of those greater than ourselves more understandable. Our intention, ultimately, is not so much to formulate a satisfactory theory as it is to find the proper orientation for seeing the first rays of the dawn of Christian hope rise above the darkness of human suffering and death.

CHAPTER ONE

Does Suffering Render Us Mute?

The Inevitable Question

On the whole, it is real, concrete, painful occurrences which acutely evoke the question of the "why" of suffering. Why, for example, does an earthquake bring down the roof of the Columbian cathedral of Popayan, precisely at the moment when more than a thousand souls had gathered under it for prayer? Must we call it "blind chance" that hundreds of them were buried in the wreckage? If these people had not "chanced" to be at prayer, they would also not have been killed. So the question arises: why does God allow something like this? Is it not actually blasphemous to use the expression "the will of God" here?

For example, how can God permit a faithful husband and father of three children to be stricken with incurable insanity just when his family needs him most? Or a brilliant priest afflicted with multiple sclerosis to visibly weaken and die young, in a diocese that is already suffering a shortage of priests? Or a young mother to lose her first child in crib death, only to find shortly thereafter that her second infant is handicapped? The Christian is inclined to ask "Where is God now?"

Why does God not listen to children who pray for their dying mother, or to wives who beg for God's grace on their weak, unfaithful husbands? Each of us can add to this list of incomprehensible blows as we please. Suffering is a problem that no one can fail to see.

People are often irritated by the fact that certain believers, especially the clergy, are all too ready to strew naive and cheap words of consolation over tragic events. "What most irritates me about you priests is the abundance of your theoretical considerations. You think you can talk away our tears, while you have no idea what the suffering of parents can mean," was the reaction of a mother to the calm certitude with which a monk had tried to console her at the death of her child.

Is there really nothing to say then about suffering? Are all words necessarily empty phrases or a mere blind? Is it true that priests and theologians have an irrepressible penchant for explaining and orating, even where silence alone is called for?

No one can deny that the Scriptures repeatedly insist on our human duty to console one another. In the Hebrew Scriptures we read, concerning the vocation of the Messiah, "The Lord has anointed me to bring good tidings to the afflicted; He has sent me to bind up the brokenhearted, and to comfort all who mourn" (Isa 61:1, 2). In fact, it is the task of all Christians to speak words of consolation to those who suffer and mourn. And is the Holy Spirit not called "the Consoler and Helper" par excellence? What sense would Christian revelation have if it totally lacked an answer to the question of the meaning of suffering? In other words, what is the meaning of any faith that remains mute when the problem of evil arises?

Yet Rabbi H. Kushner, in his recent best-seller, *When Bad Things Happen to Good People*, writes that people who are suffering "don't need theology but sympathy." So it seems to boil down, not to words (not to mention books), but to psychological support. But does not the enormous success of his book show that in fact people *do* look first of all for an answer to why so many good people are stricken by so much unmerited suffering?

Many even prefer to seek this answer from rabbis, theologians, or priests, because for them the question is always connected with the incomprehensible non-intervention of a God who apparently remains on the side-lines. The success of Kushner's theological book is proof that people in need look for more than a sympathetic clap on the back or a compassionate tear. People *do* want to know why God allows so much evil and innocent suffering.

In this book, we do not claim to offer crystal-clear solutions, let alone to present a philosophical or theological explanation. Rather, we want to lend an ear to people who experience suffering in their own body and soul and yet do not lose courage, who do not lose their joy, and who even see their faith grow and deepen. How have they borne and lived out their suffering? Why has that suffering not broken them? Can their reaction perhaps convey something to us as well, such as the way in which people best carry, understand, and interpret their cross?

When suffering strikes, all theories and pious slogans collapse like a house of cards. They even begin to sound unbearably empty. It has been justly remarked that Christian theology, for example, cannot remain the same after Auschwitz and Hiroshima. New forms of mass suffering caused new questions to arise, or at least old questions to be more sharply and urgently formulated. A mother's faith does not remain the same after her child's fatal accident. Suffering always stimulates reflection. Suffering deepens, weakens, or embitters a person, but it never leaves things as they were. Some people become gentler, more human, and more loving after suffering strikes them. Some become bitter. But no one remains the same as before. When suffering strikes, a new chapter begins in a person's life history.

A recent ad in a Flemish newspaper ran as follows: "In our family, we are searching painfully for a new balance without Joe. It is five years since our dearly beloved son and brother was taken from us. Thanks to all who continue to keep him in mind." A poignant testimonial, not only to a mother's grief, but also to the psychological shock that suffering activates within the family circle. Countless are those who try to find "a new balance" after the loss of someone who seemed indispensable to them. Alas, many never succeed. They end up embittered or discouraged. But in this book we want to consult those who have recovered their balance. We want to ask them how and where they found this new equilibrium, though not in order to imitate them as we might copy a kitchen recipe or a laboratory experiment. Faith-filled words of consolation are neither a charm nor a medical prescription. Rather, they cast new light on a problem that as such remains in existence but that can bear fruit instead of frustrating or even killing us.

Laboratories would make no sense if solutions for every problem already existed. Faith-reflections would be superfluous if the clouds of suffering and evil never overshadowed the face of God. It is not because they have found a solution that Christians believe in God. The inverse is rather true: it is because they believe in God that Christians know that suffering ultimately cannot be senseless and accidental. Christians believe that suffering must have a mysterious place in God's plan, even though they cannot always point to that precise place.

The real meaning of suffering becomes clear only long after it has occurred. This is just what is so painful in all suffering: at first sight, it looks senseless. If this were not so, then suffering would no longer be real. It would be no more than a bothersome trek towards a clearly visible mountain top.

Suffering is a mystery on which generations of believers as well as unbelievers have reflected and for which they have sought a solution. The light that some of them discovered, and the consolation that sometimes wiped away their tears, can possibly be a guide to our own search. Suffering is a mystery to which we all must seek an answer for ourselves, but we are not necessarily alone in our search.

Reflection on suffering and death cannot be relegated or delegated to third parties. Sooner or later suffering and death become a question with which God personally confronts every single person. Initially these people are often speechless. Sooner or later they discover that they are not the first to wonder about a pain that comes to them. Sufferers do not so much expect compassion as they want insight, counsel, and explanation. They want to know how others who were perhaps greater and wiser than themselves have reacted to their own suffering. If people do not do this, but close in on themselves, then they are ripe for embitterment and despair.

People need each other in suffering, even though their pain is always unique and personal. No one is called by God to carry a cross all alone. We all have our "Simon of Cyrene." On Calvary, Christ, too, spoke words, and heard words. He was not alone there, not even for a moment.

A sufferer seeking help is rightfully allergic to two things: abstract ideas that do not touch real life, and words that are purely emotional. "We do not have too much understanding and too little heart," wrote R. Musil, "but too little understanding in matters of the heart." In the Hebrew Scriptures, Job said to his friends: "How then will you comfort me with empty nothings? There is nothing left of your answers but falsehood" (Job 21:34). We should not tell a cancer patient that she looks "radiant," nor an elderly person that he is plainly getting younger every year.

Psychology and Religions

Suffering is not a psychological problem, but a religious one. Anyone who reflects on suffering outside of a religious context will readily agree that it is an insoluble problem. Psychologists look for remedies to suffering. They try to combat it, seeing in suffering the greatest enemy of the human race. The ideal of someone who only psychologizes can best be summed up by the title of the well-known best-seller, *I'm OK, You're OK.* But the believer *cannot* feel OK as long as somewhere on earth there are still people struggling on, laden with a cross.

The ideal of the believer is neither to uproot nor to anesthetize all suffering, but to make it fruitful and bearable insofar as it cannot be warded off.

The believer will follow a course between a Scylla and Charybdis which must be avoided at all cost. On the one hand, there is the exclusively psychological attitude which disguises negative realities under the slogans of "positive thinking" and "optimism." Proponents of this approach have in mind a sort of psychological comfort, mental massage, or soul-cleansing. According to these people, if you cannot say something nice and cheerful, it would be better to say nothing at all. They repress to the unconscious everything that can upset their psychological well-being. Everything shocking is hidden away. They prefer to institutionalize the handicapped; the elderly are put into a "home" where they can be "expertly" cared for. They would rather look to the beautiful and positive in this world and try their best not to let their years of prosperity be needlessly bothered.

The second rock (Charybdis) is dolorism, or the active cultivation of one's own suffering. Artificial mortifications, "do-it-yourself crosses," and masochistic practices are personally conceived and thought up under the pretext of a misunderstood "asceticism." Unfortunately, these activities have nothing to do with the true cross that is sooner or later laid on our shoulders. It is only the suffering before which we are powerless and which is therefore unavoidable that merits the name "cross."

The psychologist is therapeutically oriented. He or she wants to cure people of suffering, offering techniques by which they can face their suffering. This is a useful and extremely necessary task, as long as it is used on masochists, sadists, and dolorists (and there is a bit of these latent in everyone!). But it is a fruitless task if the psychologist tries to liberate the human condition from all meaningful suffering.

Faith relates to other problems. It wonders about the inner state of each sufferer. For the believer, suffering is not an impasse to be avoided at all cost (nor is it, on the other hand, a nice, safe place in which the pious dolorist can nestle). For believers, suffering sometimes leads to an enrichment which can be reached by no other way than that of the cross, on condition that they are not the carpenter of their own cross. Joy and pain are not necessarily mutually exclusive. Believers know that enduring happiness

never comes into being without pain, any more than the
birth of a child or the climbing of Mount Everest can succeed without hard labor. Pain is bearable only when
people see the meaning of it, or at least when they believe
it does have meaning.

A painful medical treatment which one knows is necessary for the healing process is more easily borne than a
senseless accident. In the light of faith, and most often *a
posteriori*, many apparently accidental events receive a
deeper significance. In other words, it is only later that
this person understands why a certain blow has come to
him at precisely that moment. Yet its significance never
appears clearly by means of scientific proofs or logical con-
clusions, but only when looked at against the background
of eternity, or *sub specie aeternitatis*. It is not through a better know-how with respect to suffering that believers differ
from unbelievers. Nor is it a question of greater impervi-
ousness to suffering, or more heroic courage. But believers
can relativize suffering because their horizon extends much
farther. Believers have the background of eternity at their
disposal. Believers and unbelievers alike can be stricken by
the same incurable disease. At first sight, the degree of
their pain will depend only on purely psychological and
historico-cultural factors. In fact, there are sensitive as well
as sturdy temperaments, and it is well-known that Chinese
can bear more pain without anesthetic than, for example,
Americans. What is more, in their pain, unbelievers always have the idea that "we only live once." But believers know that we do not live once, nor twice, nor even
three times, but eternally. For them, this concept casts a
relativizing light on everything that can happen to them in
this life. So, faith never lessens the pain, but projects it
against another background. Even the tallest house looks
small when it is flanked by a sky-scraper.

All great religions have wrestled with the problem of
suffering and death. What is more, they actually came
about through reflection on these problems.

For the zoologist R. Ardrey, humans differ from animals
in three respects. First, humans have a language (and not

only communication signals). Second, humans are sexually interested and excitable throughout their whole lives (and not just cyclically and in certain seasons). Third, humans are the only biological beings that are constantly and increasingly aware of the fact that they must die. In other words, humans are language-speaking, pleasure-seeking beings who by nature are confronted with the problem of death. Now, all cultures have tried repeatedly to resolve this problem in a religious context. In so doing, fetishists, shamans, or priests would come to visit the sick. This comes not from a sort of primitive naïveté, but from the notion that religion is a superfluous luxury if it has no real connection with the central problems of human life.

Buddhists strive after a Nirvana where pain and passion can no longer be felt. Taoists attune their whole lives to nature because it seems to them that it is the only way to avoid degeneration, corruption, and death. Hindus withdraw as far as possible from anything earthly, because that is associated only with decay and deception. Stoics try to remain indifferent to things of the senses; meanwhile they preach a heroic courage in the face of privation, blows, and pain. Most of all, they want to remain unmoved and strive as much as possible not to lose their equilibrium.

Judaism, for its part, wonders how the God of the Covenant, Election, and the Promised Land can be brought into relationship with the disasters that again and again have struck the Jewish people, from Egypt and Masada up to and including Auschwitz and Dachau.

Finally, for Christians, the cross of the suffering Messiah is the central symbol. This cross has quite a lot to do with the concrete life of Christians. They are baptized with the sign of the cross; they are blessed by it on their death beds. Its image hangs in their living-rooms and they are ultimately buried under its sign. The Lord says about the very life of his disciples: "He who does not take his cross and follow me is not worthy of me" (Matt 10:38). We know that the passion account is the primary nucleus of the later Gospels. The Gospels have even been called an "introduction" to the central events of cross and resurrection. The dialectic of suffering and resurrection (or of death and eternity), then, is the backbone of Christian revelation. In other words, for Christians, suffering and dying are not the last word but always the first, necessary, and providential starting point. The "dying grain of wheat" is the opening onto eternal life for us.

Whenever religion declines (as in many sectors of our modern, pagan society), psychological leaders and social experts are the ones who take over the torch of a pastoral, but secularized, approach to suffering.

CHAPTER TWO

Suffering and Theodicy

Old and New Theodicies

One of the most important functions of death is that it makes people reflect on life. One of the most important results of suffering is that people wonder about the essence of real happiness.

Just as religion arose from reflection on death, so too, theology sprang from what Leibniz has called a "theodicy": in other words, from the question, "how can we blame or justify God in view of the immense evil rampant in God's creation?"

The natural theologian or expert in theodicy, then, is first of all a lawyer who tries to clear God of the age-old charge that God has called a world into existence in which evil not only triumphs but exceeds all bounds. We can expect this theologian to explain why good as well as evil is present in the universe, yin as well as yang, angelic goodness as well as devilish machinations: in short, happiness as well as suffering.

Can't this God who wants to be called good and loving create a world without all this evil, misery, and inescapable death? Or at least a world in which the ratio of negative to positive would be less consequential?

Leibniz himself formulated the question as follows: did God create the best of all *possible* worlds? As a Christian, he was convinced that this was indeed the case. Leibniz therefore tried to explain why a material world without evil is an impossibility, at least if there is going to be room for human freedom.

Many other Christian thinkers, following the lead of Irenaeus, have shown again and again that God has created humans in a world of good *and* evil, or of joy *and* sorrow, because this is the most fruitful soil for human growth towards its true destination. Flowers grow better in fertilized soil than in a sterilized culture-dish, they say.

Other thinkers point out that we do not so much need a theodicy or natural theology as an "anthropodicy," that is, a justification of human beings who, through their evil and errors, are the direct cause of countless forms of evil in the world. Instead of asking philosophers what reasons God can have had to have mixed so much suffering and evil into the mortar of creation, this sort of theologian points out that Christ is the primary advocate of guilty humanity, which he defends against God. If evil really exists, then, they reckon, this can *a priori* come from human beings alone (e.g., Adam and Eve). Evil at least has the advantage of having made the incarnation and coming of Christ acutely necessary.

However, it seems to us, as we shall see later, that neither of these two solutions is satisfactory. We cannot load all the culpability for evil on the backs of humans. Cancer viruses, floods, or poisonous snakes are not human creations. We have even less right to use a handy philosophical theodicy to point out the "logical necessity" of suffering. From the start, reflection on suffering and death has been the first occasion for diverse religious considerations and for theological deepening. How people conceive of death and resurrection shows what they really believe (or do not believe). As Paul said: "If there is no resurrection of the dead . . . then our preaching is in vain and your faith is in vain" (1 Cor 15:13-14).

In other words, our vision of the cross and resurrection is the barometer of our Christian thought. There is a tale by the German poet Jean Paul, recounting a speech of the dead Christ from atop the world structure. The poet has Christ re-appear on earth with the disconcerting message that he "made a mistake": there is no God, alas, and so, no resurrection or eternal life either. Jean Paul goes on to describe the consternation and despair that this message effects on earth. If there is no God, then everything becomes meaningless, and as a result, everything is permitted. This is also how people react in the lives of Dostoevsky's anti-heroes.

But if Christ should suddenly appear in our time and state candidly that there is no God and no resurrection either, perhaps this news would hardly surprise many who are Christians in name only. "We did not mention it, but we had felt that this was the case for a long time already," many would perhaps say. "We knew that there was no real solution for suffering and death. That is why we have made of it what we could." Such Christians have already sought their private salvation in a more psychological approach and they have been living for a long time already *etsi Deus non daretur* (as if there were no God).

To be sure, much has changed in the "Christian world" in the last hundred and fifty years. Indifference has often replaced discomfiture with ultimate questions. To realize this, we have only to listen to how Christians (even the clergy) console the suffering and the dying. Does Christ's cross and resurrection still come spontaneously to their lips? Don't they prefer to be less "dramatic," stressing more up-to-date treatment for the dying, or resorting to a purely sociable friendliness? So in suffering and death they do what medicine does in "hopeless cases": they choose to stick to pain-killing, because they no longer believe in a solution. Suffering and death lead either to religious deepening or factual unbelief. What T. S. Eliot says about travel is also true for suffering: "Those who travel are never totally the same when they come back." This brings out the need to stand still a bit *before* departing on this journey.

When we are standing before the abyss of suffering, there are two attitudes that are detrimental: to fall hopelessly into it, or to close our eyes in fear of spiritual dizziness. There are many and diverse guides on the human path of suffering. We can opt for a purely psychological approach. But in this book we especially want to cast light on the Christian perspective, even though we may compare it with various other ways of thinking which sometimes seem more courageous, but which seldom are more lucid.

Suffering: The Heart of Faith

The whole history of theology and spirituality demonstrates that new religious insights sprouted only in fields previously cultivated by serious problems and painful struggles. What heresies were to dogmatic theology, the problem of suffering has been to spirituality. "The most precious insights into the human situation were not discovered through peaceful introspection or systematic research, but always through the shock of dramatic mistakes," said the Jewish philosopher A. Heschel. "It is continually in moments of deep frustration, crisis and self-disappointment that a person comes to radical reflection; seldom in moments of enthusiasm over one's own accomplishments" (A. Heschel, *Who Is Man?* [Stanford, 1965] 14).

On a scientific level, too, it seems that the greatest inventions often occurred in periods of war and distress. (Think of penicillin, radar, jet planes, atomic energy, rockets, etc.) Pain in all its forms has forced us to reflection and required us to look for new possibilities. Suffering stimulates human creativity.

It also touches humans in their faith. Suffering literally cuts through our most cherished principles and notions. A twenty-year-old idealistic scout-leader, left crippled as a result of an automobile accident, evolved in only a few months from a believing activist into an embittered cynic. On closer inspection, it was apparent that his faith had not disappeared, but rather it had turned into a virulent rebellion against God. This is not an unusual, though painful, development. It is a reaction which makes one think of the Jewish author Elie Wiesel, who as a fifteen-year-old youth arrived in a concentration camp. There he lived through the death of his father and of all his friends.

As the sole survivor, he later testifies, ''Never shall I forget the little faces of all those children whose bodies I saw go up in billows of smoke. Never shall I forget the flames that have consumed my faith for all time. Never shall I forget the night silence that forever deprived me of all desire to go on living. Never shall I forget the moments that killed my God and my soul and made all my dreams go up in ashes. Never shall I forget these things, not even were I doomed to live as long as God Himself. Never'' (E. Wiesel, *Night,* [London, 1958] 45). Wiesel, it is true, did not doubt the existence of God—witness his later writings. But he did refuse to give God any belief, credit, or trust, because he could no longer see what such a God could have to do with love, fidelity, or the Covenant. The shock of suffering never has automatic results. Rather, the shock places the victim before a new choice. The further course of one's life depends on it. That this choice does not have to be either simple or blind is something we want to make a bit more clear in this book.

On a purely human, interpersonal level, sufferers stand before new options or choices. The young parents of a handicapped child often come to the realization, in their painful challenge, that in the care for this child (and in the socio-psychological difficulties that result from it in their milieu) they will either grow closer to one another, or else will become strangers, disagreeing over the question of what exactly has to be done about it.

Suffering (such as sickness, natural catastrophes, pain, etc.) must be combatted with all ethically permissible means, where it is at all possible. Where it is not, people cannot refuse the suffering by putting a stop to life. Radical but immoral means toward the elimination of suffering (or of seeing others suffer) are, for example, euthanasia, abortion, or suicide (in other words, forms of ''total anesthesia'').

The duty to combat suffering wherever possible implies, for one thing, that we ought to prevent suffering as much we can. Chain smoking, excessive use of alcohol, neglect of one's own health (e.g., by enslavery to work), spoiling of children through love of ease or weakness, are only a few practices by which people seek their own unhappiness, as it were. On a more spiritual level, those who throw their belief in God overboard must not complain later if they suffer from the *mal du siècle* or from the meaninglessness of life. Just as a stuntman brings both his health and his life into unnecessary peril, so, too, heedless, unthoughtful marriage partners visibly throw themselves right into their own misery, even though, naturally, they are seldom conscious of it. Just as fever can be a warning of infection or of an unhealthy way of life, so, too, a painful misfortune can be a sign that one has taken a wrong turn in life.

Avoidance of unnecessary suffering does not mean developing a sort of phobia for suffering, or regarding suffering as public enemy number one. Probably more people are psychologically crippled by anxiety about suffering that may come their way than by actual suffering itself. They are more concerned about the future than about the present. The word of Christ, "Sufficient for the day is the evil thereof" is exchanged for the slogan, "Avoid all decisions that might have painful consequences." The mass media and advertisements make clever use of this "anxiety about the future." Think of the systematic exploitation of the fear of obesity, cholesterol, or carcinogens; the craze for insurance against all imaginable calamities; the forms of thrift that degenerate into miserliness; or the "prudence" that leads imperceptibly to radical egocentrism.

The poet Auden called our culture "the age of anxiety." In fact, people seem less and less psychologically resistant to the menace of adversity, pain, and failure. The reason is plain. People no longer look on inevitable suffering as a "cross," that is, as a passage-way or bridge leading to the Promised Land, but rather as a blind wall against which their life has crashed, as in a twisting labyrinth.

Suffering is the only bridge that leads across from the shore of temporal "having" to the land of eternal "being." The Dutch poet E. Hoornik, speaking of the spheres of having and being, writes:

> Having is nothing. Is war. Is not living.
> Is of the world and its gods.
> Being, lifted up above these things,
> Is filled with divine pain . . .
> Being is the soul, is listening, is yielding,
> Is becoming a child and looking at the stars
> And being slowly raised up beyond.

"Having" always stands in relationship to things that can be concretely described and enumerated. "Being," on the other hand, has to do with persons with whom one enters into relationship. Being is a question of "degree of humanity," which increases to the degree that relationships deepen. Life circumstances can make us more human. But, unfortunately, they can also lead to inhumanity. "Having" has to do with possessions and ownership. "Being," on the other hand, has to do with values and persons.

It is striking that our manner of "being" grows only in the degree to which we let go of our possessions; in other words, our being human grows to the degree that we dare to come down from the pedestal of our possessions. For many, the shock of suffering is the occasion to leave the pedestal they once owned and to see with new eyes what life is all about: in a word, that we live in order to approach the Other.

The core of the Christian message can be summarized in psychological terms as follows: I become myself only through my relationships with others (*inter alia*, with the Divine Other). My motives for approaching others can be of a triple nature:

—the pain of my own neediness or solitude;
—the pain that I read in the eyes of others asking for help;
—the irresistible charm that goes out from the others whom I meet.

The first two contacts are brought about through a cross. The third is called a "grace" in Christian perspective. The cross, too, can be a grace when one knows how to place it rightly on one's shoulders and does not flatly reject or refuse it.

Finally, how does one dare to write something on the meaning of suffering without being an expert in this matter? Is it not all too easy to multiply words about realities that one has never experienced in the flesh? The answer is perhaps that a doctor does not have to have cancer to be able to stand at the side of a cancer patient. A judge does not have to be divorced in order to make a fair judgment about a divorce case. Perhaps most patients even prefer a healthy doctor. Naturally, however, no one is perfectly healthy, just as there is no one who has absolutely no idea what suffering is. Many people, unfortunately, have never known true happiness, but there is nobody who has never been confronted by *some* misfortune.

That is why we will venture—albeit in cautious and modest fashion—to present a few considerations on forms of suffering that we ourselves have never experienced. Just as every cancer specialist knows that cancer is still incurable, so too everyone who writes anything about suffering knows that suffering itself is not thereby resolved, but remains a mystery as unsoundable as Godself. The fact that God is, and always shall remain, a mystery does not mean the end of theology, however. On the contrary, it is the only reason for theology's continued existence.

CHAPTER THREE

Three Kinds of Suffering

Physical, Psychological, Social

No two people live out their love-life, or their solitude, in exactly the same way. Every love-story is unique. Likewise, no path of suffering is comparable to any other. Just as there are many forms of the friendship experience or of solitude, so too there is an infinite range of human suffering. We must distinguish at least three kinds of suffering: physical, psychological, and social.

Like every pain, suffering that is purely corporeal or physical is very subjective and scarcely measurable or experimentally verifiable. Not only are there people who are hypersensitive; there are others who can grin and bear it. Not everyone is equally quick to reach for pain-killers or anesthetics. Animals can suffer only physically. But in the case of humans, physical pain is always linked with mental suffering. For example, a cancer patient who is undergoing physical pain perhaps suffers much more by knowing that her disease is incurable and that she is going to leave four children motherless.

The two most important forms of psychological suffering are anxiety (e.g., on account of an operation, an examination, loss of a job, etc.) and gradual isolation (e.g., after the loss of a friend, a spouse, or a child).

Finally, "social" suffering is what we call the agony of knowing that one is cutting a poor figure in the eyes of society. Bankruptcy is accompanied by many materially painful consequences, but many experience it more (some even primarily so) as a shameful dishonor or a disgrace to their name. Their prestige suffers because of it; they feel out of the purview of their earlier trusted circles. This can be purely imaginary on their part; in many instances they are the victims of their own spontaneous withdrawal.

In the primitive Catholic Church, public sinners normally underwent the three afore-mentioned forms of pain: physical penance, psychological guilt (which sometimes degenerated into a wild growth of scrupulosity), and social excommunication from the ecclesial or sacramental life.

Christ also simultaneously experienced these three forms of suffering on the cross, and in a most acute way: physical bleeding to death from his wounds, together with slow asphyxiation; the psychological realization of the betrayal of his own disciples who, except for a few women, fled, and even a feeling of being abandoned by God; finally, the social ignominy of being executed between vulgar murderers as a common rabble-rouser and would-be prophet, an execution that brought his whole message into discredit. For Christ did not die as a heroic martyr proudly witnessing to his faith to the last. Christ died as a common criminal. His death was a total degradation, humiliation, and apparent failure. His suffering was three-fold, and thus total.

In the Modern World

It is striking that the three afore-mentioned forms of suffering have radically increased in these last centuries. Modern people cannot withstand physical pain, psychological suffering, and social failure as well as earlier generations could.

In fact, physical suffering is a "metabletic," or historically evolving, phenomenon. People of the Middle Ages withstood more pain than we moderns, primitive African tribesmen more than North Americans, and soldiers in Stalingrad more than Düsseldorf or Frankfurt bankers. As the psychiatrist J. Van den Berg wrote: "Historically, pain has increased sharply since the beginning of the nineteenth century." According to him, this increase of the physical sensation of pain can be explained psychologi-

cally. The more individualistic and solitary a person becomes, the keener the attention concentrated on awareness
of self. Busy homemakers have less time to be concerned
about their own discomforts or to take their own tempera-
ture than do confirmed bachelors. This is also why groups
or nations with a strong feeling of togetherness have a
greater capacity for survival than do independent loners.

A French surgeon from the First World War front, R.
Leriche, testified that sensitivity to pain was altogether
different among Asians and Africans than, for example,
among Germans and French. The hardiest of all seemed to
be the Cossacks: "When Russian officers confided to him
(the surgeon) that it was really superfluous to put Cossacks under anesthesia for an operation, he noticed that in
fact he could amputate parts from hand or foot without
anesthesia and without the patient showing any sign of
pain" (cf. J. Van den Berg, *Leven in Meervoud* [Nijkerk,
1963] 253 and 256).

Psychological suffering has also increased markedly
across the ages. The loss of a child has always been a
painful event for a mother. But we must not forget that *before* 1800, we can find scarcely a single family in which
parents saw the death of fewer than half their children.
Before the spectacular progress of medical science and of
economic welfare (i.e., *before* the nineteenth century in the
West, and later elsewhere), the death of a few children
from a well-to-do family, and even more from less well-
endowed families, was an ordinary and inevitable occur-
rence, inherent in life itself. When Ann Stuart became
queen of England, Scotland, and Ireland in 1702, all her
seventeen children had already died. This did not hinder
her later from reigning single-handedly over what was
then the mightiest realm on earth.

As the infant mortality rate declined in the West, its
tragedy was also more and more felt. The more frequently
doctors succeeded in saving children, the worse it seemed
that they did not manage to save them all. The more the
death of people in their prime of life is successfully avoided,
the more difficult it is today to submit to the inevitable.

Fewer and fewer parents lose their children now, but we also find that if they do, they are more marked by it. This is understandable, but at the same time it shows how acutely the depth of psychological suffering increases as its frequency decreases.

The French historian J. Delumeau studied the historical growth of anxiety-feelings in the Western soul throughout the last centuries. In a second work, he went on to examine the role played by the Church in the conscious stimulation of anxious guilt-feelings. "Spiritual leaders of the West have done everything they could to exchange the heavy collective anxiety that was weighing on people because of a whole chain of stressful circumstances (e.g., the Black Death, the Hundred Years' War, the "Turkish Peril," etc.) for theological objects of fear" (J. Delumeau, *La Peur en Occident* [Paris, 1978] 23). For pedagogical reasons, people's feelings of anxiety were redirected toward objects considered more worthy of them.

Instead of being afraid of things of secondary importance, people would be better off, according to their spiritual leaders, if they paid attention to "real" dangers. It seems that people are always laden with a dose of inescapable anxiety, but the objects of this anxiety can evolve historically. In our day, too, we are experiencing a shift in our feelings of anxiety. Popular preachers of earlier days used to make people afraid of dangers that threatened the *soul*. Modern dietitians, doctors, and popular prophets of health have now taken over the relay: they instill fright about possible dangers to the *body* (think of hypertension, lung cancer, pollution, etc.). People show what they honestly believe in or what they truly value by what they really fear.

The soul has ceded to the body, eternal future to the immediate present, and conscience pangs to fear of social failure. Meanwhile, in our Western world, anxiety is increasing every year. The reason for this is two-fold. The more refined a civilization becomes, through a rich cultural past and steady technical progress, the more fragile are the people who live in it, and the more aware they become of the dangers threatening them. The more they have to lose, the sooner they look for a security system. There is a direct correlation between the notion of possible dangers and people's cultural level. A deer is much more skittish than a fly. Secondly, when people no longer view death as a transitory phase, but rather as a disastrous terminal station, the classical objects of anxiety (sickness, old-age, and death) produce all the more anxiety. The decline of faith is paid for by a higher toll in "metaphysical anxiety," as Gabriel Marcel calls it.

Just as bodily pain and psychological suffering cause depressions or melancholy, so too social suffering causes a feeling of humiliation and failure. But "success" in modern society is constantly harder to come by, because of increased competition, and so the much-desired success is all the rarer. In other words: fewer and fewer people find their pleasure in society. More and more people feel frustrated, cheated, or insufficiently appreciated. "Social suffering" is increasing in our times.

By "social suffering" we mean not only the fact that certain races, groups, or classes feel shoved aside or humiliated (e.g., blacks, homosexuals, linguistic minorities, or the handicapped) but also the fact that even "normal" people are afflicted with the fear that they will not "make it" in the arena of modern society, and that they will not get their just due.

Society is regarded as a "race-course" and its athletes are under heavy stress. They know that in a race there can be only one winner, and that the public is totally merciless. An acutely increased *Geltungsdrang* (drive for self-affirmation and self-worth) moves modern people to tormented anxiety about failures. Because they do not feel that they are "somebody" yet, they seek advice from technicians of success. These experts first lay out for them how their body has to appear (e.g., tanned, slender, young, athletic, even relaxed), what forms of relaxation will become "musts" for them (e.g., jogging, surfing, hiking, cycling, etc.) and especially what techniques they must use in order to create a more favorable impression than the competition (e.g., speak a foreign language fluently, have traveled and experienced a lot, subscribe to modern ideologies, etc.).

Society has really become a "stage" on which people move about like nervous actors with stage-fright, afraid of the judgment of the audience, afraid of having to be content with a supporting role, or worse yet, simply afraid of failing in their role. The scenario of their lives is no longer prescribed by the gospel, not to mention the person of Christ, but by the "world," that is, by a number of psychological producers and social directors. The priests and servants of salvation of previous times have been replaced by "engineers of social success."

Christ's Response to Social Suffering

Diametrically opposed to this stand Christ's message of poverty of spirit and his admonition to those rich in successes. The unmistakable growth of social suffering is especially to be attributed to the inability of so many to believe in anything more important than theatrical success or social applause.

Poverty of spirit can assume various forms; for example, misjudgment by the public, or failure, against which the world is forever warning us in an anxiety-producing way.

Indeed, there are more painful forms of poverty than a financial or material shortage. Some people dispose of five talents; others must carry on with only one. For the social set, this latter fate spells disaster. But Christ, on the contrary, calls it "blessedness." For him, it is a positive power, at least if people do not grimly bury their one talent in the ground and stubbornly refuse to use it. Guardini has justly called the Sermon on the Mount the "reversal of all values." What the world deems catastrophe, Christ calls "blessedness." And those who are exalted at the world's hands will hear words of warning from Christ.

So there are, for example, people with remarkable health as well as others who must live their lives with a handicap, a weak psyche, or a severe injury. Modern pagans care for nothing so much as their health and psychological balance. For Christ's disciples, however, there are more important values.

We find people with pleasing faces, harmoniously shaped bodies, and attractive appearances. They immediately catch our eye. But next to them live less striking people, suffering from a disturbing birthmark, obesity, a physique which is too tall or too short, an unpopular hair-color, or whatever characteristic one pleases. They suffer because of it. They feel the eyes of others constantly on them. All of this gives them a feeling of being "lesser." It is a feeling that sometimes weighs upon them like lead. That, too, is a form of spiritual poverty, which can cause grave psychological suffering.

Next to the young with a future before them stand the aged whose time seems definitively past. Nowadays, youth carries the trump card, whereas the elderly feel more and more pushed aside. In other words, there are also people who are poor with respect to the numbers of years they have ahead of them. And for the elderly in our times, growing old betokens social suffering that was largely unknown to previous generations.

There are highly moral people with irreproachable conduct. For many, they are a model and a cause of pride for their family members. Beside them, and in their shadow, we find the "publicans," the weak or notorious sinners, those of whom Christ said: "Those who are well have no need of a physician, but those who are sick; I came not to call the righteous, but sinners" (Mark 2:17). Nevertheless, most superiors, leaders, or parents prefer, for understandable but not necessarily evangelical reasons, disciples who are faultless, charming, and good. To feel the finger of accusation or the raised eyebrows of the "perfect" directed against oneself time and again can be a form of social suffering.

Finally, in our families and cloisters, we find people with an almost self-evident prayer-life, side by side with others who, in their spiritual poverty, must say with the apostles, "Lord, teach us to pray!"

All these examples of poverty can betoken a handicap in the "great theater of the world." In any case, even though they are a "social pain," they can still be a fruitful cross for the kingdom of God. It is about those who suffer in this way that Christ says: "Blessed are those who mourn, for they shall be comforted."

The more the modern world accentuates accomplishments, success, and competition, the greater the suffering of those who think they come up short in all of this (most especially for those who have no notion that behind this world-theater there lies a world that is much more real, relativizing everything). Those who glide out onto the slippery stage of social success have two exits. Either this shock wakes them up and turns them back to reality. They rub their eyes and wonder astoundedly why they busied themselves so much for something that was ultimately nothing more than a theatrical act. Mostly, they discover there is something in this life more important than the possible reaping of transitory applause. Or else they react in the opposite way. With a blush of shame on their cheeks, they get up and try to resume the thread of the drama. They always think they read feelings of mockery or pity in the mirror of others' eyes. They feel inferior. It is true of social suffering, too, that it either deepens or frustrates a person. But it leaves no one unmoved.

CHAPTER FOUR

Culpable Suffering
and the Suffering of Others

The Pelagian Mistake

Human suffering can be divided into physical, psychological, and social suffering. We must also make a distinction between suffering caused by people (e.g., concentration camps, spoiled children, accidents caused by joy-riders, etc.) and unavoidable natural catastrophes (e.g., perennial drought, serpent bites, or hereditary disease). To put it more theologically: there are forms of suffering that are the result of human sin, as well as others that spring inescapably from "original sin." We will speak more at length of "original sin" or "natural evil" in the next chapter. Here it must suffice to note that "original sin" is an infelicitous term, attributed to Augustine. Infelicitous, because it has nothing to do with any "sin" at all, but is rather a condition into which everyone is born; it is not a hereditary matter carried over through sexuality or birth, but rather an ontological mode of being in which the whole of reality lies anchored.

A brief word about the suffering that people continually cause others must suffice here. Like Marxists, some contemporary liberation theologians often give the impression that our world could become a paradise on earth if only people would behave a little more justly and humanely with each other, and, more concretely, if only social and political relationships could be reorganized. In their eyes, *all* evil emanates from human beings themselves and thus not from the nature of things or from matter. They are

"Pelagians" who believe in the fundamental goodness of primitive people (still undamaged by private ownership and inequality). All evil then would come from false societal structures. Not so much religious as political considerations are the order of the day. The task of religion is reduced to an evangelical inspiration that is supposed to lay the axe to the misshapen trees of feudalism, capitalism, middle-class mentality, etc. As Rousseau says: "It is inequality of living conditions [and thus not original sin] which has awakened ambition, jealousy, betrayal, etc. in the primitive soul. In their constant struggle against the poor, the rich have deftly forced a political contract on them, in order, so to speak, to defend the weak, keep the imperious under control, and to guarantee each person their just possessions" (J. J. Rousseau, *Discours sur l'Origine de l'Inégalité,* 1755). We are familiar with the famous slogan of Rousseau: "Human beings are fundamentally good, but it is society that corrupts them." Just like all "Pelagians," Rousseau and his later disciples *over*rate human guilt and its institutions while they *under*rate natural or "original" evil. In other words, they are utopian with regard to social planning, and romantic or idyllic with regard to the nature of primitive, unspoiled aborigines. For centuries, Christian theology, however, has taught that the "natural" human contains much evil as well as much good. This is why "natural" persons need "supernatural" or divine help if they are going to reorganize their environment, which is indeed their first great task. They must not only improve political structures but first of all themselves, that is to say, they must manage to get their *Geltungsdrang* (drive for self-affirmation) and their natural desires under control.

All later disciples of Rousseau (e.g., Marx, the anarchists, and a certain type of liberation theologian) localize social evil in one type of human being: the powerful, the Establishment, Westerners, Capitalists, etc. The poor, the oppressed, and primitives meanwhile enjoy the status of "immaculate conception." But Christian tradition on this point is more pessimistic: with the exception of Mary, *no one* is conceived and born without hereditary stain. As a result evil is at home *everywhere* and *everybody* is sending *someone* to the devil from time to time.

In any case, liberation theologians and nature-enthusiasts, in addition to many others, have quite correctly directed our attention to a very wide-spread sort of suffering that can indeed be attributed to human guilt, and which can and must be helped with social, psycho-therapeutic, and political treatments. While moralists and preachers used to lay the primary accent on individual guilt and private evil, modern preachers of penance point with wagging finger to social evil, immoral structures, and their results "here below." *Both* forms of evil are, alas, important.

Yet the distinction between evil caused by humans and that flowing from the nature of things (thus, between guilty and innocent—or unavoidable—suffering) is not as sharp as people might think. Both forms of suffering are very frequently interwoven with each other. We are indeed powerless against the infertile, scorching drought of the Sahara, but a centuries-old Turkish-Arabian egoistical deforestation project has a lot to do with it. So, too, the drought and the famine of northern Brazil or of the Sahel cannot be ascribed to purely meteorological conditions. Nature created by God *needs* and is meant for human, cultural, creative intervention. When this does not happen, that is, when people "let God's water flow over God's dikes," fertile farmland becomes a swampy morass.

This is also true in the instinctual life of humans. Natural instincts require moral self-control; if they are not controlled, what is deeper in human beings never comes to full development. We often hear it said that modern sexual inflation, unbridled self-affirmation and ambition, and even an increasingly self-defensive, egocentric tendency all "proceed from human instincts" and thus are "natural." The argument continues: a person should not interfere too much against these "natural" tendencies; otherwise, he or she ends up with frustrations and complexes.

The logic behind this is always the same: human nature is fundamentally good (and thus not burdened with original sin). One should, then live according to nature (not following any "supernatural" or religious principles). People all too easily forget that the instincts (drives) created by God, such as sexuality, self-affirmation, and ambition, stand in service to something more essential. For example, sexuality is a "language" given by God in order to promote deeper, stronger contact between human beings. Thus, sexuality is *more* than a handy pleasure-arouser. It *can* awaken pleasure when natural impulses have come into the service of a higher value; red roses are beautiful in themselves, but they receive a wholly new meaning when I pluck a dozen of them and send them to my beloved.

All natural drives—no matter how positive they are in themselves—can get out of hand, become disordered, and therefore become destructive in an "anti-natural" way. This happens when we lose sight of the fact that even deeper, though less noticeable, desires are harbored within us, such as a desire for God, eternal life, the discovery of ultimate meaning, etc., things about which a superficial person seldom bothers. Repression of the higher desires in a human being leads to hyper-activity of the lower drives. Those who deny religious hunger end up with imbalanced excesses in other areas.

The "deprivation syndrome," so frequently observed by biologists among animals that are encaged or living in artificial conditions, also happens very frequently in the spiritual realm among human beings. Animals that are hindered for a long time from satisfying a certain instinct (e.g., a caged sparrow which does not get a live fly to eat, or an isolated steer that has not had access to a cow for weeks) will show an abnormal nervous tension and a dangerous aggressivity. Likewise, among human beings spiritual desires can remain unsatisfied, and even become totally unconscious. Many so-called "natural" or spontaneous excesses are nothing but the warning symptoms of an anti-natural neglect of deeper needs.

Suffering caused by humans can be physical (e.g., torture, automobile accidents, medical error, etc.), psychological (e.g., anxiety about nuclear stockpiling, over-population, increasing crime, etc.), or social (e.g., loss of honor, calumny, dishonest competition, etc.). Such suffering can be alleviated by better policies of criminology, political revolutions, better-adapted psychological direction, and better methods of teaching: in a word, by human sciences. But as to suffering that is unavoidable and inevitable: here the treasure hidden in the field will never be found outside the realm of faith.

To what degree are humans responsible for the suffering they constantly inflict on their fellow human beings? On the one hand, it seems that modern people have become much more liberal, and on the other hand, much more strict. In the cases of individuals, all sorts of mitigating circumstances are brought to bear; in the case of structures and organizations, the critique is becoming more and more radical and less nuanced. People who commit crimes of passion, kidnappers, terrorists, etc., are examined by understanding psychiatrists and often defended as naive idealists. The rich countries, the multi-national corporations, the Church, capitalism, etc., however, are treated mercilessly. People no longer seek the cause of evil so much in the human soul as in structural deficiencies or political bungling. Organizations are considered more important than individuals, who are supposedly only toys for them. The conversion of the human person is not thought to be as important as the reform of social institutions.

In reality however, every individual is a *laboratorium beatitudinis* (as the Marxist E. Bloch puts it), that is, a laboratory in which the greatest possible happiness must be sought. This happiness must be found on both the personal and the social level. Here we must mention that this happiness does not consist in a utopian elimination of all suffering and pain, but rather in a fruitful integration of them. In any case, this is the core of the Christian message of the Cross.

Suffering from Misguided Love

Let us make a final distinction between our own suffering and that which touches others, especially the others who are our "neighbors" and about whom we are deeply concerned. It is well known that mothers are more affected by the suffering of their child than by their own pain. To put it more precisely, they themselves are stricken by the suffering that comes over their child, a phenomenon that is proper to all true love-relationships. Now with regard to this, we can make two remarks. We can never love another too much, it is true; but we *can* love the other in a wrong way. Secondly, another's pain always remains a much greater mystery than our own. These two considerations demand a bit of clarification.

Exaggeration in love is really impossible. Love can go down the wrong path, however. It can become too maternalistic, grasping, or intrusive. Thus it can degenerate into a possessive drive and as such be the source of much unnecessary suffering and countless disappointments. On the other hand, love can want so badly to prevent evil in the other that it inhibits the other's freedom by wanting to make decisions in his or her place. It can thus degenerate into passionate attachment or excessive concern. In both cases, the result is unnecessary pain.

A requirement in all adult love is an acceptance that my partner is (and becomes) other than what I had supposed and especially other than what I had dreamed. Simone Weil speaks about our foolish and sterile desire to "want to be the personal creator of what we love," whereby we want to imitate God, as it were. We want to shape the object of our love and to give it form according to our own opinion, inspiration, or hierarchy of values. This is how it can happen that not only does the victim of our affection understandably withdraw from our intrusive interferences, but also that God takes away the object of our concerns.

"To live purely means: to accept a certain distance. This means to respect the distance between oneself and the beloved" (S. Weil, *La pesanteur et la grace* [Paris, 1948] 19, 70, and 71). In this sense, God sometimes "purifies" our human love by creating a ''distance'' when that love risks getting lost, and by creating ''space'' for a higher good. In connection with the subject of people who remain heart-and-soul attached to others and to ''alien things,'' Ruusbroec, speaking of God, writes: ''Because He is not yet able to give Himself and His gifts, since they (humans) do not yet desire and want them, He often rouses fire and robbery against them, so that they might recognize Him and understand their blessedness'' (J. Van Ruusbroec, *Werken*, vol. 1, [Tielt, 1943] 50).

Suffering and Compassion

The reason for suffering that touches us is a mystery which the following chapters will treat somewhat more deeply. The reason for suffering that touches others, on the other hand (e.g., friends, relatives, or strangers with whom we feel a solidarity) is an even greater mystery. In both instances, the veil of this mystery is lifted only slightly in the light of faith. The faithful do receive, sooner or later, some insight into the meaning or sense of what happened to them (ordinarily only after the painful events themselves; were this not so, then the events would certainly no longer be so ''painful''). But we can seldom or never expect to see through our neighbors' fate, for everyone's life is at least partly a secret between themselves and their God. Thomas à Kempis writes about others' suffering: it always remains ''a secret judgment of God that we will never fathom. It transcends human judgment and no study or discussion can expose this divine judgment'' (T. à Kempis, *The Imitation of Christ*, III, ch. 58, v. 12).

We know the admonition Christ gave to Peter when he began to be concerned about his friend John and therefore raised the question, ''Lord, what then about him [John]?'' Immediately Jesus made it clear to him that the vocation of one's friend or fellow human ultimately remains a mystery that concerns only God and that person: ''If it is my will that he remain until I come, what is that to you?'' (John 21:21-22).

Yet it cannot surprise anyone that a good mother remains concerned about the fate of her child. She will even
live vicariously the situation in which the child finds itself.
Perhaps she might manage to console herself with the
thought that in raising and caring for a handicapped child,
the initial shock ultimately deepens and enriches her. But
then what about the innocent child itself? For example,
what is going to happen with this child when Mother is
no longer there? How difficult it is to see and understand
that such a heavy cross can result in good for her child!
Theories can no longer avail here. But a concrete example
can bring some light to the question.

Teilhard de Chardin has often been accused of an innate
tendency to naïve optimism. The fact that he never yielded
to this undeniable characteristic at decisive moments was
something he owed to his dear handicapped sister, Marguerite. Whenever he spoke, wrote, or reflected on suffering and failure in God's creation, he always kept her in
mind. Without the existence of Marguerite, and without
his special affection for her, Teilhard would certainly have
written much differently about the evil in this world. She
gave him a greater attentiveness and deeper sense for concrete reality. She was the one who inspired him to write
one of his most remarkable works, *Sur la souffrance (On
Suffering)*, as well as to compose some of his most profound letters.

Moreover, the prayer and the psychological support of
this handicapped woman mattered a great deal to him. In
brief, by her being handicapped, Marguerite played an irreplaceable role in the thought as well as in the concrete
life of Teilhard. What Teilhard has meant and will continue to mean for many Christians could never have come
to pass without the regular confrontation of this great
savant with his sick sister.

The suffering of others calls forth two essential reactions
from good people: on the one hand, zeal and help, and on
the other, compassion. With regard to zeal, we should
avoid stubborn intrusiveness caused by too great an attachment. We must not detach or separate ourselves from

others, but we must learn to adhere to them in a new, perhaps purified, way. Most of all, we are called not to attach ourselves to them in an exclusive manner. In a certain sense, believers attach themselves to everyone and everything, insofar as people and things are placed by God on our life's path; this is not by accident. Most importantly, we should not lose sight of the final goal. Let us be more attached to this "final goal" than to all the rest.

Love is not a condition of the heart but an orientation of the spirit and of the whole person. In other words, love is much more than "being in love." Love is an orientation to the Other. God often removes objects which might obstruct our view of Godself. The objects of our love are never annihilated; rather, they are shifted. They can no longer stand in the way, and are therefore, each in its own mysterious way, called to God.

Compassion with the suffering of others is, above all, a question of not falling asleep. We must remain awake, present to the other. As Bergson says: *Dormir, c'est se désintéresser* (falling asleep signifies a lack of interest).

"Compassion is a wound of the heart," says Ruusbroec, "that rouses love for all people, and it can never be healed, as long as there is anything good in a person; for above all virtues, God has charged us with compassion in mourning and pain" (J. van Ruusbroec, *Werken*, vol. 1, 128). In Gethsemani, Christ must have missed this sort of compassion from his chosen friends.

CHAPTER FIVE

Natural Evil or "Original Sin"

Finding the Middle Ground

In addition to evil caused by humans, there is another sort of evil that comes directly from the very nature of things; besides the suffering which is the result of human failings (or sin), there is also a suffering that arises from the partially negative situation into which everyone is born. This negatively charged situation is what Christians call "original sin."

As a consequence, much of this world's suffering is not merely the result of not living according to divinely created nature; something has apparently gone awry with nature itself. It is therefore impossible to draw the conclusion as to what is good or evil by beginning with human nature and the nature of things (as Orientals often do), for in the Christian perspective, nature has a hereditary taint; it is partially corrupt or at least certainly not that for which God called this nature into life. "In the name of no other doctrine have so many people been killed," said Anatole France, "as from the idea that the human being is naturally good." With its teaching on original sin, the Church has always wanted to emphasize that by nature there is indeed much good in humans, but also a great deal of evil. In the animal kingdom we note that there are not only deer, horses, and nightingales, but also tse-tse flies, scorpions, and rattlesnakes.

Yet Christians are not as pessimistic as Manichaeans, who think they find a second power in the world, evil and independent of God: a demonic power against which God is actually helpless. We can understand the attractiveness (and cheapness) of such a view: all the suffering and evil in the world can now be charged to this evil anti-God or devil. Good alone is God's concern. God gets white-washed. He means extremely well, but even he has to reckon with evil that even with the best intent cannot be removed from the world.

Diametrically opposed to this pessimistic view stands another heresy: Pelagianism. Pelagians are fundamentally optimists and activists. The existence of the devil, original sin, and unhealthy tendencies in human beings is simply denied. Nature is fundamentally good, and the evil principle totally eradicable, provided people only have good will. Therefore, supernatural interventions are superfluous. We do find unavoidable suffering in the world, but that suffering is no more than a dialectical moment, necessary for the universal synthesis or cosmic reconciliation of the future. In other words, for Pelagians, there is no "garbage" in creation; nothing gets lost, and nothing is really evil. In fact, modern atheism and the militantly anti-Christian humanism of the Enlightenment are extreme forms of Pelagianism. In this view, ultimately God is not needed; humans can manage their affairs very well on their own. If they only know how to extend themselves and use all the powers of their nature, then any divine intervention, redemption, or mediation is superfluous.

Again and again, the Christian Church has tried to steer its course between Scylla and Charybdis (Manichaeism and Pelagianism) in their ever-new forms. Manichaean-oriented Christians show a tendency to think conservatively. We can do nothing, they affirm, against evil in the world. Therefore, we should flee as far as we can from the world and its temptations, and place our ultimate hope in the hereafter. Modern Pelagians, on the other hand, are especially to be found in the ranks of the more progressively-oriented, secularized, and politically active Christians. They believe in a world that can and must be improved by human effort, without sounding the alarm of the supernatural. "Not Lourdes, but science; not prayer, but social action!" runs their motto.

According to them, our oversize burden of suffering is caused by human error and guilt; evil must therefore be combated by human action and will power. Rome also sees Pelagian tendencies in the optimistic admirer of the positively-evolving universe, Teilhard. He brushed dangerously close to the rock of a sort of Pelagian pantheism because of his admiration for nature and his dislike of defeatism and spiritual inertia.

In the eyes of Luther, all Roman Catholics were out-and-out Pelagians who thought they could improve the world and merit heaven by their own accomplishments and merits. Luther continually reproached Catholics for their "works righteousness." He himself accentuated human corruption (i.e., original sin) on the one hand, and on the other, the unmerited grace of God which alone sanctifies.

Remarkably enough, it was the Polish philosopher Kolakowski, an expert on Marxism, who pointed out that the essential values of our whole Western culture would be threatened if the Church were to yield to the growing temptation to give up the doctrine of original sin and the reality of the devil (L. Kolakowski, "Kan de Duivel Verlost Worden?" in *Essays van L. Kolakowski* [Utrecht, 1983] 86).

What, precisely, is meant by these two notions, "original sin" and "devil," which are sometimes thought archaic and hereditary?

God's Demand for Creativity

First of all, the doctrine of original sin means that there is more evil in the world than can be explained by human guilt alone or resolved by human effort. As Paul says: "We are not contending against flesh and blood, but against the principalities, against the powers" (Eph 6:12). Evil and suffering constitute a reality which can be noticed in all of nature, and which is simply not empirically explainable, let alone soluble.

Some naïve theories have been suggested, whereby God would have created the cosmos from the very beginning in a paradisiacal and perfect condition, where suffering and evil were totally absent. Human sin would then have disturbed this harmonious condition and at once opened the gates to a landslide of misery. And then Christ would have appeared on the scene to rescue what was still salvageable of the original plan and artistry of God. But Christ did not come into the world in order to restore a primitive order (which, by the way, never did exist), but rather to give orientation and stimulation to human development and "hominization." In Christ it has been made clear for humanity who God is, what it really means to "be human," and to what glory God has destined us. Instead of an "original sin" we do better to speak, in the footsteps of Teilhard, of a very difficult and time-consuming beginning. Instead of "redemption," we speak of liberation; and instead of "expiation," we speak of a progress which will inevitably cost much suffering, tears, and failures.

From the outset, all humans were born into a world in which anxiety, pain, suffering, and death were undeniable and unavoidable realities. Since Christ, we know clearly why God allowed this state of affairs, and even considered it necessary for ultimate salvation. The divine Creator is not a restorer or curator of broken pots. God creates "from nothing." We were created according to God's image in order to be "creative" too. We do not create "out of nothing," it is true, but from matter that is far from perfect or finished. Everyone of us must model our art-work, our life-work, out of clay in which both good and evil (or joy and suffering) are intermingled. This is what it means to live our vocation. No two people get the same *materia prima* to work with. There are some who set to work with five talents (and of them much shall be required), and there are others who have to row their boat with only one talent.

The paradise of Eden is not the description of something that used to exist. Rather it is a first sketch or project of what God has in mind for us forever. This plan, then, can only be achieved by difficult conquest and transformation of the evil in this world. God did not set these difficulties in our way in order to test us, to punish us, or to try us, but in order to unleash our creativity, originality, and uniqueness. A mother can give her child a lovely book printed in colors. Or she can give that child a simple coloring book. In the second instance, the child itself must hold the crayons and go to work. Here the child must do nearly everything, but that is what in his eyes is precisely so exciting and thrilling. Without this difficult process of coloring by himself, in spite of many blots and mistakes, the child would never come to a sense of respect for a perfectly successful painting.

Original Sin: The Evil in the World

The cosmos created by God is the iron ore from which the dross of evil can be removed only by a fire that requires effort and suffering. It goes without saying that this process of creation, to which we are all called, is from the very beginning limited and interrupted by human sinfulness. Sin and negativism are, as it were, "second nature" for us. They lie anchored in our very nature. This is why it makes sense to speak of an "original sin" or "archetypal guilt."

Not only matter itself but also the human psyche contain negative elements. They must be channeled by morality and spiritualized by religion. In other words, people must not only build dikes against floods; they must also form their character and establish moral principles in order to control the voluntary drives latent in their nature. To be born in a situation of original sin means that in addition to many noble things in human nature, we also find aggressivity, egoism, anxiety, and every sort of tension.

"Why do Europeans so often call Americans naïve?" wonders French sociologist M. Crozier. "Why do so many American dreams, since Vietnam, Watergate, Kennedy's death, etc., seem to be suddenly dreamed out?" In his book, *Le Mal américain*, he points out that Americans really

never did believe in the existence of evil. After having believed firmly—for more than two hundred years—in progress, democracy, technology, and the limitless
possibilities of the future, Americans (who up till then always localized misery, stupidity, and retardation outside
their borders) suddenly became acquainted with evil hidden within the American way of life itself. America had
never believed in fundamentally perverse tendencies in
humans, in nature, and in society itself.

This is why a psychiatrist such as C. Rogers was such an
out-and-out optimist. His counsel: "Affirm and encourage,
but never give directives or critiques!" These latter lead
only to inhibitions or frustrations, he thought. The successful child psychologist, B. Spock, recommended an
anti-authoritarian approach to thousands of parents. Not
long ago, he admitted that the first generations of adults
who had grown up as "Spock-babies" did not seem at all
as happy, optimistic, and well-balanced as he had
dreamed and predicted. Today's malaise, according to
Crozier, is the result of the fact that Americans never took
seriously the reality of evil in themselves and in others,
and therefore were not prepared, for example, for the
shocks of Vietnam, Watergate, or Dallas.

On the other hand, Europeans "have been used to seeing evil everywhere. Our whole culture and everyone's
personality were constructed with evil taken into account.
In our eyes, our children, for example, are beings in need
of a culture . . . For centuries, we have learned that we
have to tame evil (in the world and in ourselves). That is
why we Europeans are so complicated and so problemati-
cal, but that is why we also succeed better at finding an
answer to this basic problem. In our culture, sin is still
considered a reality" (M. Crozier, *Le Mal américain,* [Paris,
1980] 283).

Here we are not talking about whether Americans are
less Christian or less realistic than Europeans. Both have
their advantages and disadvantages (and converge notice-
ably toward each other). But those who think that nature
is totally good and that it therefore must get every chance

for spontaneous development will quickly learn that they are mistaken. Whoever lets nature run its course will soon have to reckon with weeds, parasites, and underbrush.

Belief in original sin means acknowledging that our biological mechanisms and innate tendencies do not of themselves lead to solidarity and fraternity the moment our defective political institutions are overturned by revolution and our superstitions dispelled. Evil lurks within human beings themselves. In all of nature we find warning tendencies. In order to correct this evil situation, more is necessary than political improvement and religious aggiornamento.

"Original sin" is the sober affirmation that even our noblest deeds contain elements of stubbornness, ambition, or envy, that good on earth is seldom entirely good, that the gold of our best intentions never attains the twenty-four carat level, that instances of holiness are not frequent.

"Original sin" also means that none of us can totally free ourselves from the shadow-side or the imprint of our past. Our birth was already a traumatic event, and the first sound we emitted was a painful wail, which calmed down only when, as nurslings, we first lost consciousness and fell asleep.

"Original sin" means that every good is mixed with evil, except in the person of Jesus Christ, the "new Adam." The liberating message of Jesus Christ is that this situation can not only be fruitful, but that, in the long run, it will even appear necessary for human happiness.

The doctrine of "original sin" is a double religious affirmation. On the one hand, evil and suffering are omnipresent in the divinely-created universe; on the other hand, any and every cooperation with this evil is sinful. But God wills only good. Evil is never God's intention. God never willed the death of the Just One; therefore God awakened him from death (and along with him, all who ever were, or ever will be, victims of suffering and death).

That suffering and evil can be found everywhere in this world (and thus not only in guilty people who are disturbed, defiled, or unbalanced by nature) is also the sober affirmation of zoologists as well as of anthropologists and psychologists.

"The world of animals is a world full of fear and anxiety," writes the ethologist R. Ardrey (R. Ardrey, *African Genesis. An Investigation into the Animal Origin and Nature of Man* [London, 1961] 62). In other words, it is not only domestic animals, bred, used, and ultimately slaughtered by humans, that experience pain, anxiety, and misery. We should foster no romantic illusions about wildlife either. Animals fear, spy on, and kill each other. For the rest, it is noteworthy that the problem of animal suffering is seldom, if ever, touched on by philosophers and theologians. What can be the meaning of suffering among beings that disappear completely in death? Perhaps among animals, as opposed to humans, the individual is offered up for the good of the species. In other words, an animal's life can be called successful if the evolution of the species benefits from it or through it. Moreover, the animal exists for humans who naturally are able to use or misuse, respect or destroy, ennoble or exterminate it. But this problem falls outside the scope of our consideration.

Nobel Prize winner K. Lorenz wrote a famous, authoritative book on the instinct of aggressivity in both animals and humans. As a biologist, he calls this instinct a "so-called evil," because the drive for fighting and killing can and must play a positive role (even though it easily gets out of hand) among both animals and humans. This drive, which has already undeniably caused much suffering, seems to be a "necessary evil" in the anthropogenesis or evolution of animals into human beings.

"What makes humans unique among all primates is the fact that for thousands of years they alone were totally dependent on systematic killing in order to survive," says R. Ardrey. They had a "natural predisposition" to it because of three factors: "walking erect on two legs, free use of their hands, and the invention of weapons" (R. Ardrey, *The Hunting Hypothesis* [London, 1977] 16, 42). Without a strongly developed instinct of aggressivity, humans would have been wiped off the map long ago. In their nature itself are hidden violence, destruction, pain, and the death-wish. But this evil is a necessary factor for making the good possible. Evil has a meaning. It plays a role.

Yet these evil tendencies easily degenerate (as do all in-stincts) when they are not controlled by reason, namely, by the moral rules-of-the-game and conscience. At least this is the case with humans. Moreover, humans stimulate their instinctive desires for eating, drinking, sexuality, and violence by artificial means (for example, by appetizers, saltine-crackers, aphrodisiacs, demagogy, violent films, etc.). This is why E. Fromm distinguishes two distinct forms of human aggressivity (just as there are also varying forms of sexuality, desire for food, etc.). The first is a "defensive, mild sort of aggressivity, in service of one's own life-preservation as well as that of the entire human species. It ceases as soon as the external threat is gone. The second type, however, is terrible and destructive, and proper to the human species . . . It is insane and only aims at greater lust" (E. Fromm, *The Anatomy of Human Destructiveness* [Greenwich, 1973]).

All natural drives are a gift from the Creator. But they can degenerate into sin as soon as they become "dis-ordered," that is, no longer controlled by conscience, the "thermostat" of the understanding. Concretely, this means that instincts become disordered when they are no longer in the service of higher desires and values.

Humans are biological beings, but at the same time, they are also much than that. That "more" (the soul) has its needs and wants, too, even though this latter is always calling less loudly for liberation than the lower instincts do (so that many are not even aware of these higher desires). Thirsty people in the desert hanker after water, just as a lion hankers after an antelope or zebra. But no one "hankers" after a Mendelssohn violin concerto or a half hour of silent prayer. Culpable evil or sin arises by an "in-flation" of lower instincts, which always brings in its train a real devaluation of the higher desires.

The Devil: Negative Power

Finally, the authors of the Bible made a connection between original sin and the power of evil, as personified in the devil. Think, for example, of the story of the Fall and particularly of the meeting between Eve and the serpent. Since the Middle Ages, the concept of "devil" is unfortunately laden with the most naïve, bizarre, and anthropomorphic associations. Here is not the place to go into a sort of theology of the devil, or demonology. But it would be an indication of intellectual sloth if we would leave the question untouched, as so often happens in theological circles, just because modern people find it "so hard to take."

No one can deny that the Jews in the Hebrew Scriptures as well as Christ in the Christian Scriptures speak emphatically and often about the devil, whom they regarded as an active principle in the cosmos. The Christian conviction that there is a devil in the works rests upon two considerations. The first is humanistic; the second is a question of purely human common sense. But first, let us note that the question "whether we must believe in the existence of the devil" is senseless, because "belief" has to do only with a person one loves and in whom one trusts. Either the existence of the devil is a reality that forces itself on the experience and reflection of a thinking person, or else one leaves the problem outside consideration. It is possible to become holy and never consciously have met up with demonic powers in this life.

From the humanistic perspective of Christian revelation (that is, from its deep respect for the phenomenon of the human being, God's favorite creature, of which "God saw that it was very good") we are taught that people have brought about more evil in the world than can be explained by the ill will of these people themselves. When we look over the battleground of all that people have done to each other, and are still doing, in the course of the centuries, purely human motives do not offer a satisfactory explanation for this immense power of destruction. Already in the story of the Fall in paradise, a third actor en-

tered on the scene with Adam and Eve under the symbolic
form of a serpent. The mistake both of them made cannot
be explained solely from the perspective of human arro-
gance and stupidity. How were the Holocaust and the
Gulag Archipelago possible when psychologists correctly
assure us that people basically mean well and that they
are merely seeking happiness, however clumsily and mis-
takenly they might go about it? Because of our respect for
human beings, Christians assume that people are sometimes the instrument of invisible non-indigenous powers,
which at times "possess" and influence these same
people.

The Bible gives the name "devil" to these mysterious
powers which "surpass flesh and blood." Unfortunately,
later generations of Christians, yielding to a childish and
naïve inclination for fables, ascribed characteristics of
"flesh and blood" to this invisible power and thus
declared them "visible," at least in certain frightening circumstances. The result of this was that many intelligent
people not only threw overboard these late-medieval
fables, but also went on to deny the very existence of invisible negative powers.

Besides this, there is yet another thought-provoking affirmation which concerns purely human understanding.
Many Jews and Christians (in addition to Manichaeans,
adherents of Zoroaster, etc.) seem to have felt and understood in their own life in certain circumstances that they
were sometimes crippled by a mysterious force that over-
came them in their actions and strivings. With Paul, they
must sometimes say, "I do not understand my own actions. For I do not do what I want, but I do the very thing
that I hate" (Rom 7:15). People cannot of themselves say
much about this mysterious force of evil. It cannot be
localized or listened to with the stethoscope of psychological science. If we want to get to know something about it,
then we must go to divine revelation. Christ himself called
this power "a liar, the father of all lies" (John 8:44). Thus
it is a force that thrives exclusively in a climate of untruth
and in turn it produces only more untruth. In other words,

where truth is trodden underfoot, or where even the *existence* of a truth is denied (for example, by the motto: "Each has his own truth"), we can apply the word of the Jewish psalmist: *Abyssus abyssum invocat*, or, "yielding to evil automatically leads to worse evil."

Against this force (which, as we shall see later, plays a positive role in God's plan and which is a reality, even though without ontological autonomy), he steps into the breach, he who says of himself: "I am the Truth" (John 14:6). This is why Tolstoy's witness is so typically Christian when he writes, "What I love most on earth is truth."

Acceptance of the existence of the devil (or of "demons," in the expression of Dostoevsky) is thus a question of humanistic good sense and a phenomenological spirit of observation, two virtues which unfortunately are not highly listed in the market of contemporary sensibilities.

"The presence of the devil confirms that evil is an integral part of the world, and can never be totally banished from it," according to the expert on Marxism, Kolakowski. "And so we must not reckon on a universal (or total) reconciliation" (L. Kolakowski, "Kan de Duivel Verlost Worden?" 86). Consequently, not everything that exists will be taken up into heaven. Besides heaven there is also the real possibility of a "hell" or conscious refusal.

God respects human freedom so much that God gives us the possibility to refuse Godself.

CHAPTER SIX

Is God's Power Only Relative?

God's Self-Limitation

Shortly before her death in a concentration camp, the Jewish woman Etty Hillesum jotted this marvelous prayer into her diary: "One thing is getting clearer and clearer for me: that You [God] cannot help us, but that we must help You, and in that way, we help ourselves . . . . Yes, my God, it does not seem that You can do much to the circumstances; they now match this life. I am not calling You to responsibility; You may call us later to responsibility for it. It gets clearer to me with almost every heartbeat: that You cannot help us, but we must help You, and we must defend to the utmost the dwelling in ourselves where You live" (E. Hillesum, *Het Verstoorde Leven*, Dagboek van 1941–1943 [Haarlem, 1981] 131, 132).

In fact, there is something that God cannot do, namely, to create a world in which love, creativity, and freedom would be possible, but in which there would be no suffering. For without suffering, these three central pillars of human life are excluded. Love can exist only as long as dissatisfaction and "passion" are real. Creativity presumes deficiencies and imperfection; freedom implies the possibility of wrong choices, or sin.

If you say A, you must also say B. If the Creator brought into existence a world in which people are to be capable of love, inventiveness, and personal resolve, then the world cannot be a spiritual wonderland in which everything continues to run smoothly and in which misfortunes are in principle excluded.

Thus, F. Varillon writes, "God respects us too much to spare us all suffering by using magical interventions. And He respects Himself too much to spare Himself any suffering-on-account-of-our-suffering . . . . The work of creation is an adventure. God dared to undertake this adventure. He paved a way of freedom for humans, a way flanked by dangers" (F. Varillon, *L'Humilite de Dieu* [Paris, 1974] 124; idem, *La Souffrance de Dieu* [Paris, 1975] 16).

In other words, suffering becomes a necessary ingredient, if we regard love, creativity, and freedom as necessary. In a world in which there is no room for suffering and dissatisfaction, desires cannot exist. Those who have everything no longer desire anything. Desire is the essence of love.

Suffering and Love

There are two reasons why love and suffering are related to each other. Love is always born from a feeling of lack and incompleteness, and love always requires sacrifices.

What a loving person experiences above all is that, because of the absence of his beloved, he is missing something. He then feels imperfect and incomplete. This feeling is at once his pain and his richness. The lover says: "Without you, I am nothing; I feel empty and hopeless." Strangely enough, this feeling first arose in him at the first meeting with his beloved. She evoked in him a passionate desire and awakened his hunger, both of which were previously unknown to him. For love does not satisfy any needs (as sexuality most often does). Instead, it *causes* desire that can even become "passionate." One who is missing his beloved feels in a certain way even more lonely than someone who has no beloved at all (and who, as a result, has not the faintest idea what he is missing). It is because loneliness is possible that love can become such a deeply human experience. Love changes the pain of loneliness into a new and "richer" pain, namely, an insatiable yearning for the other. This yearning causes pain because the other, in spite of everything, always remains an "other" with whom I will never be fully one. This strange feeling is verbalized by the poet-psychiatrist M. Vasalis:

> Sometimes, when you are silent and looking out your window
> your beauty seizes me like despair,
> a despair no consolation can extinguish,
> as great as my own existence, and just as old.
> That I must see you and cannot BE you
> separated from you by my own eyes
> that you are sitting there, so much outside myself,
> it pains me like a birth.

Buddhists try to escape pain by escaping to a Nirvana where pain, desires, and passion cease. But for Christians this pain is something precious and holy; it causes them to increase their search for the Other (who can be God or a human being). Once people have tasted of God, they will better realize how truly the earth, in spite of every-thing, is still a "vale of tears."

Here, Hadewijch would have spoken of a "winter land-scape," John of the Cross of a "night," and Ignatius of a "desert." Only one who has once seen the sunlight knows how dark a night can be.

There is a second reason for love to be related to suffer-ing: it brings sacrifice with it. Every parent who brings children into the world knows this, just as every friend knows that a true bond implies responsibility and every monk realizes that cloistered life is more than religious satisfaction. In a certain sense, each person is "crucified" to his friend or partner. As soon as one in love under-stands *more* than a certain emotional state (e.g., of being in love) or a periodic satisfaction of lust, then such a love will presume sacrifice and commitment. Christianity considers love, with sacrifice, as central.

What Christians call "Providence" is, among other things, God's inviting presence in all the needs of the world. Indeed, we still hear loud cries for help here on earth. There are still many needy people, especially our "neighbors" who look at us longingly, not so much on account of their riches and success as because of their neediness, pain, or loneliness. Suffering and neediness make people long for each other. It is not as though God would use the rich as a cure-all for the needs of the poor. Rather, the inverse is true; the needs of the world are so indispensable because they create the occasion for many to become committed to self-giving.

Only in giving do people become themselves. In a world in which everything runs perfectly and smoothly, personalities do not blossom. People develop only in situations in which much needs to be done. From the suffering of the world, God gives each person his or her vocation and task. "The harvest is great, but the laborers are few." And yet people do not exist for the harvest. Rather, the harvest is the only place where people can arrive at self-development, that is, true humanity.

Suffering and Creativity

In a world without suffering, creativity is also excluded. The true world is a "laboratory" in the etymological sense of the word: a place of work and sweat. There is no place where new solutions are so eagerly sought after as where people are faced with acute difficulties. We can think of the battle against cancer, new sources of energy, the problems of overpopulation, etc. The painful difficulties with which people and cultures are continually being confronted seem to be the most powerful incentives for scientific research, economic planning, and political renewal. Creativity is a dike which people erect because a river of suffering is constantly overflowing the field of their lives. In a world devoid of suffering and evil, creativity would immediately be superfluous.

The search for new forms of humanness (e.g., regarding home construction, experience of marriage, or care of the handicapped) is meaningful because there are still a number of imperfections in the concrete world in which we live. Present suffering is the motive for what Teilhard has called the "process of hominization."

In his book on suffering, dedicated to his favorite sister Marguerite, who was handicapped, Teilhard writes that "no progress is conceivable in the world without its toll of tears, blood, and sin." He calls it the "complementary mechanism of good and evil" which is a "universal phenomenon." "By this law of God's creation, even the most obscure and repulsive suffering becomes . . . a supreme means to the hominization and divinization of the universe . . . . The growth of the spirit is born from a shortage of matter" (P. Teilhard de Chardin, "L'Activation de l'énergie," *Oeuvres* vol. 7 [Paris, 1963] 256–257). Human creativity is, as it were, a transformer that starts working only through the current or tension of suffering.

Naturally, we can ask why creativity or the art of novelty is a necessity for us. For Christians the answer is clear; God has created humans after his own image, thus after the image of a creator. One builds oneself up by a multiplicity of options. A personality is the result of a series of choices or preferences between what is valuable and what is not.

Heredity, the past, and circumstances of life do partially determine a person, but they do not hinder personal inspiration. Rather, they are the outer decor in which the spontaneity of the ego must develop its own life history. They are the providential scenario that by no means excludes a personal shaping and lifestyle, but rather makes them possible. I cannot change what is inevitable in my life. But I certainly can give a value and meaning to it. I do not need to create this meaning myself; I have to seek for it as for the "treasure hidden in the field."

Creativity is possible only when there is a natural resistance to the good, the beautiful, and the true. This is why a sculpture in oak or marble is much more beautiful than one in fir or plastic. These latter materials do not offer enough resistance to the artist's chisel. God not only puts resistance to creative intervention in nature itself, but also in the hard living conditions with which each person is sometimes confronted and in the internal struggle some have with their own difficult character and temperament. The human will to live stands in great need of such resistance in order to develop its own originality.

Pampered or spoiled children seldom have to deny themselves anything, or exert any effort, for their parents remove every potential obstacle from their lives. The most common result of this is boredom and loss of initiative. The divine Father never "spoils" his children. Because of original sin, a person finds herself in a life milieu strongly resistant to what is good; therefore the art of living well and formation of character become all the more necessary. It is well known that where there is the greatest wealth, the will to live is ordinarily the weakest (and the amount of suicide and chemical-dependency the largest). In Egypt, for example, the percentage of suicides is particularly low (0.3 per 100,000 people). But in Sweden, the paradise of social planning, the suicidal rate is the maximum: 18.6 for every 100,000 people.

God has given us a world in which good never comes easily. Instead, we are given the heavy assignment to concretize the good. Every plant we sow is quickly surrounded and threatened by many natural weeds and parasites.

When Christians daily pray, "lead us not into temptation," they know assuredly that it is God who has created all those "tempting" things. God—and not the devil—is the creator of the many attractive things that so often make our choice and fidelity so difficult. After all, the fruit tree and the serpent that seduced Eve were creatures of God. In the garden of our lives, God has created not only a number of difficulties and burdensome tasks, but also dangerous and tempting things. These latter so easily draw our attention away from essential realities that some people flee them totally, even deep into the Egyptian desert, or behind the walls of an enclosed monastery.

Why has God made us in such a way that we naturally hanker after things that can be harmful to our physical and spiritual health (e.g., alcohol, tobacco, foods, wealth, comfort, lack of exercise, etc.)? Why has God created, in the garden of our lives, so many fascinating things from

which we are then asked to abstain? Why taunt children's
eyes with things they are not supposed to touch or will
never get? The answer is clear: because love is not possible without choice or selection. In order to choose, there
must be at least various possible objects to choose from,
only one of which will be preferred and become a reality.
In marriage, a man does not choose his beloved because
all other young women are ugly or are out of reach for
him, and certainly not because there simply are no other
women. In that case, the "choice" would be easy, and
any pain of hesitation and risk excluded. Think, for example, of organized marriages between total strangers in
the sect of Reverend Moon.

Choice always has to do with predilection. Many things
speak to my heart and enchant my eyes. Because of this,
my definitive choice for someone is actually the highest
honor I can pay this person (the choice of marriage, religious vows, faithful friendship, etc.).

If the tree of good and evil with its forbidden fruit had
not been in the earthly paradise, that is to say, if there
had been no possibility of sinning, error, or infidelity, then
Eve would at once have become sub-human. Without
creativity, she would not have been able to let her instincts and nature run their natural course.

Where sin is impossible, creative freedom is not only
superfluous, but also excluded. If physical and moral evil
did not exist, then good deeds, personal preference,
creativity, and love would also cease to exist. The fruit tree
created by God was thus not an absolute evil, that is, it
was not evil in itself; instead, it was an attractive "lust for
the eyes." God does not create evil as such. (Moral) evil
consists in a wrong choice between things that are good in
themselves. In turn, asceticism is not a good in itself. It
takes on value only if we in giving up a lesser good set
our eyes on a greater good. The true ascetic is content
with nothing but the best. In this sense, asceticism is precisely the inverse of sin.

Sin or moral evil consists in a disordering of our life of
love. A husband who loves his secretary more than his
wife and a pastor who pays more attention to his wine cel-

lar than to his parishioners are living immorally. Yet, the secretary and the wine-cellar are not bad things in themselves. By their choices, people not only show who they are; by their choices they build up their personality and become who they are.

Character is what certain values that fascinate a person (e.g., money, sports, career, children, God, etc.) have made of him or her. Like Adam and Eve who walked in the garden of Eden, selecting and plucking its fruit, we are strolling through a God-created garden, in which we have to choose again and again between good and less good. To choose the lesser good is to do evil. Every tree has its importance in that garden. Not a single bramble bush or weed is superfluous.

In the past, certain well-intentioned clergy repeatedly tried to hide the tree of good and evil, and especially the forbidden fruit, for the sake of safety. So, until recently, people thought it safer if religious sisters, brothers, and priests would not go to films, theater, sports stadiums, swimming pools, or the beach, so as not to be unnecessarily tempted by apples not meant for them. Women religious were to leave behind, in all humility, any plans for further university studies. Clergy were supposed to wear very noticeable, long, black cassocks. Moreover, sisters had to wear a conspicuously complicated veil by which public missteps would be, if not altogether impossible, at least less likely and less easy. They went about, not in sackcloth, but in a conspicuous (witnessing) uniform. In a word, they were given a "stigma." It was hoped that they would not even get a glimpse of the tree of good and evil. They were neutralized by showy control-mechanisms. Excessive freedom and originality were thereby avoided—a situation which makes one think of Dostoevski's Grand Inquisitor, who said to Christ: "Freedom, free spirit, and science will land them in a maze . . . . Instead of making human freedom superfluous, You have expanded freedom and encumbered the human soul forever by torments inherent in freedom . . . . Instead of simply obeying the clear law, from now on, man must decide for himself, with free will, between good and evil" (F. Dostoevski, *The Brothers Karamazov* [Brussels, 1970] 257, 261). In other words, instead of letting them walk in a garden from which all attractive but dangerous trees were removed, You, O Christ, have wanted people to be in a garden in which they could, and must, choose between what is good and evil for them.

Lastly, human creativity is also stimulated by anxiety about failure. The existence of failure has a positive function, for if everyone were to succeed automatically, no one would really make an earnest effort. Without the erection of barriers, no horse would ever succeed in the high jump. The barriers are not set up in order to bar the way, and certainly not to make the horse stumble, but rather to spur it on to a brilliant jump.

Naturally, at times people set the bar too high for the horse, so that it rears up or, in the worst case, breaks its neck. And so, we also find teachers who overload their pupils, or parents who discourage their children by excessive demands. But Paul writes, "God is faithful and He will not let you be tempted beyond your strength, but with the temptation will also provide the way of escape, that you may be able to endure it" (1 Cor 10:13).

Suffering and Freedom

When speaking of "creativity," we are also speaking of "freedom." As in the case of love, so too creativity and freedom are possible only when the human being is not irresistibly or involuntarily drawn towards the good. Freedom is not only possible but necessary if lesser goods or unnecessary and even disturbing things fascinate a person. The quintessential free choice which confronts everyone in this life sooner or later (and sometimes again and again) is the option for or against God, or rather, to be with or without God. This freedom does not mean that it makes little difference *what* one chooses. The option for or against God is "free" because the choice must be made by the person herself or himself. This option, then, has nothing to do with inherited behavioral patterns or learned automatism.

"Your yes is of value only if a no is also conceivable," says Schelling. Well, never has a "no" to God been so conceivable as in our days. Doubt about God's reality has nearly become a status symbol of a modern, critical, or progressive spirit. To have no problems with religion is easily considered old-fashioned and naïve. There are indeed serious problems, but they are also salutary. The function or the importance of these problems consists in the fact that they make a free and personal reflection necessary. In fact, there are good arguments both for and against belief in God. There are clear signs which show that God is active, present, and discoverable in this world. But there are just as many signs that make us doubt God's love and even God's existence.

The clearest of these "negative signs" is certainly what concerns us here: the existence of so much innocent suffering and unmerited evil. Those who are sensitive to suffering in this world find the existence of a loving God no longer so evident. "The non-evidence of God is really a necessity," contends Simone Weil. "If God were more evident, then He would inevitably crush all His creatures." In other words, "no" would be impossible, and "yes" would be inevitable, instead of a free, personal act. If God showed himself to us, even for one instant, in full reality, then we could do nothing but run to God as a bee instinctively flies to nectar or a moth to light in the darkness. But faith is not an instinctive reaction to an attractive religious incentive. Faith is a free act. As Simone Weil says, "We need an outlook on the world in which we could also encounter emptiness, so that God would be able to fill this emptiness. That presupposes the existence of evil" (S. Weil, *La Pesanteur et la Grace*, [Paris, 1948] 21; cf. also 46).

The German psychiatrist A. Görres writes: "If we would find it hard to breathe every time we left off prayer or religious practices, or conversely, if any thought of God would be immediately rewarded by a feeling of pleasure, taste, or liberation, then conceivably everyone would promptly become a believer. But that sort of belief would rather be like the behavior of conditioned rats" [A. Görres, *Kennt die Psychologie den Menschen?* [Munich, 1978] 127).

The lack of any pain when we abandon God and the lack of any immediate feeling of pleasure when we pray make it possible for people freely and unconstrainedly to turn to God. Prayer is not a means to find gratifying mental feelings or peak experiences. If a lamp goes out, then mosquitoes, fish, or moths quickly disappear from the environs. If God's self-evidence falls away (as is the case in our time), then only the conventional believers disappear from the ecclesial community. In this way, the rest arrive at a more adult faith. God loves the *generous* giver, one who loves freely and without constraint.

"God can do all but one thing," writes the Orthodox theologian Paul Evdokimov. "He cannot oblige us to love Him." In fact, love that is obligatory or commanded is a contradiction in terms. God does not impose himself on us. God wants to be sought. God most frequently hides himself behind the reality of suffering and evil. The darkness in which God often wraps himself in this world is necessary in order to make possible the joy of personal discovery and encounter. Our attentiveness to God or our faith is not the result of an innate spiritual balance but of a discovery, an encounter, even a revelation into which one can enter or to which one can refuse to respond.

Even though our faith is the result of an encounter with God, this assuredly does not mean that God is an "object" or a "being" that we glimpsed on a certain specific day, and in whom, as a result, we began to believe.

First of all, God is *spoken* of. God does not come to us by way of an apparition, a light or a shock, but by way of a word. God is spoken of by a mother who teaches her child to pray, by a catechist who prepares confirmands, or by a preacher who explains the gospel to the parishioners. Faith arises where people speak of God, or hear someone speak of God. God can be brought into our speech in many ways: in positive or negative ways, in contemporary

or old-fashioned ways, in Christian or Muslim ways, etc.
But people can also keep silent about God.

"There are people who probably never would have
fallen in love had they never heard anyone speak of
love," writes La Rochefoucauld correctly. In the same
way, most believers might never have discovered God had
they never heard anyone speak of God. Few people meet
God in our time because God is spoken of so seldom, or
so clumsily, or so one-sidedly. We experience now what
Martin Buber called "a temporary black-out" of God, a
religious eclipse.

But the painful darkness and spiritual privation also
have an important positive function. Religious suffering, or
the "night of the soul," has a meaning. Isn't spring so
delightful and new precisely because of the long winter of
apparent death that preceded it? Doesn't a prolonged
silence create attentiveness for a liberating word? Perhaps
God was far too long on our lips in a self-evident, banal,
and cheap way, so that people today wait for a word that
will be born from an authentic encounter. Perhaps that is
why the mystics at present are finding a growing audience; they are not describing any "things" or dogmas
about God. Their word is simply the fall-out of their encounter with God.

Love, creativity, freedom, and faith thus take root in a
ground from which evil and its many consequences have
only recently been weeded out. Evil seems to be an indispensable raw material in the laboratory in which we all
seek after the best formulas for our future and for our
happiness. This certainly does not mean that we may see
suffering as a "means" to achieve something positive, and
certainly not as a means that we ought to construct on our
own, or synthetically (e.g., as penance, mortification,
mutilation, or any sort of created form of suffering).
Suffering becomes dolorism or masochism as soon as we
make our own crosses instead of taking up the cross that
is laid upon our shoulders. The cross does not *make* sense;
it *gives* sense to everything. Suffering is never a value in
itself. But where it is unavoidable, it gives a depth to love,

it forms a springboard for creativity, and creates space for freedom. Of these three values, love, according to Paul, is surely the most important.

Asceticism is not a prophylactic means for safeguarding love, and least of all, for creating it. Asceticism is only the inevitable result of a love which has already come into being. Neither the fidelity of a spouse nor a priest's celibacy is achieved by ascetical rigor; rather, when marriage or celibacy is lived seriously, out of one's understanding of vocation, sacrifice is the inescapable consequence.

This sacrifice or self-denial is not a masochistic means of proving, increasing, or stimulating love; rather, it is the consequence of love born of an encounter. As Ibsen said, "What makes friendship so precious is not everything one has to do for one's friend, but that which one has to leave undone for the friend's sake."

The price of all human and religious love is ultimately paid in the coin of tears and pain. Because many no longer want to pay this price, true love has become a rare bird of an endangered species. It is for this true love that freedom, creativity, and faith will always be indispensable.

CHAPTER SEVEN

Making Human and Divine Sense

Faith or Despair

For the free-thinker and philosopher J. Kruithof, people are the "meaning-givers" of everything in existence. In itself, he holds, the world is meaningless and arises out of a series of coincidences. But because meaninglessness is unbearable (especially where illness, suffering, and death are concerned), a person must give a meaning to what is really absurd in itself.

A. Camus takes this logic one step further. His book *The Myth of Sisyphus* begins with these words: "Basically there is but one single philosophical problem: suicide. To decide that life is or is not worth the trouble to live is to answer the fundamental question of philosophy" (A. Camus, *Le Mythe de Sisyphe* [Paris, 1945] 15). Camus' answer is clear: life is really meaningless. Yet, according to him, a person may not commit suicide. Rather he must muster up his courage to bear the absurdity of life heroically, and hold out.

People of faith subscribe to the position of Kruithof and Camus that we are essentially "meaning-givers." However, we must discover and receive this meaning, not create it ourselves. For us, God is the answer to the question of who the human being is. That answer comes, not from the human brain but from the existence of God. If there were no God, then all the negative things in this world would indeed be totally meaningless. But God "reveals" to us in Christ that what is apparently absurd is in reality full of significance, and even precious.

For an atheist such as Nietzsche, all religious meaning-giving is a "vital illusion" that makes miserable lives bearable. For Marx, it is a form of "spiritual opium" or illusory happiness in the midst of life-conditions which cry out for vengeance. According to him, the anesthetic effect of religion can be so great that the religious person no longer even feels the need to revolt against his circumstances of life.

Christians, too, regularly taste the bitter flavor of meaninglessness in the things of this life. True, a great deal of suffering at first sight appears absurd: a debilitating handicap, an early death, or the suffering of an innocent child, etc. But in these chronic bursts of despair, Christians experience that an answer is offered them in God's revelation, especially in the person of Christ. Here it is a question, not of treating psychological wounds with home-made bandages, but of the word of God that seems to be an answer to the great human questions.

That word of God is not a magic formula appearing on the computer-screen of the mourning heart or the praying spirit. The real meaning of suffering reaches a person via these channels: meditation on the Scriptures, the witness of many other believers who have themselves wrestled with the great questions of life and death, and the apparently accidental situations in which people find themselves—circumstances which will later appear "providential." In other words, there is something "sacramental" in the word of the Bible, in the witness of the mystics, and in the concrete difficulties which we all sometimes see ourselves facing. For Christians, the meaning of suffering is a gift of God which we can accept or refuse. This meaning is never a construction of purely human, intellectual creativity

In brief, we can put it this way: in suffering, Christians see, not "blind fate," but rather the sharp eye of an all-provident God. We do not first discover that our suffering is meaningful, and then, as a result, conclude that God must exist. Believers' reasoning runs just the opposite: because they know (and sometimes even experience) that God is an almighty and loving reality, Christians admit that their suffering *cannot* be meaningless. Its meaning is seldom clear in the beginning. Usually, it is clear only after the most severe pain is already over. Suffering does not prove the existence of God, but the existence of God implies that suffering does have a meaning. As a result, Nietzsche and Marx are mistaken when they think that those who suffer are the only ones to discover God. It generally takes a while before human faith is faced with the trial by fire (i.e., suffering). Suffering does not create faith (indeed, the opposite is true). But suffering consolidates and purifies an already existing faith, while it blows away immature and primitive forms of faith like chaff in the wind.

Where there is no faith, suffering leads to despair. Where faith is too shallow, it does not survive the trial by fire, and it collapses. Where it is genuine, no matter how imperfect, it is strengthened.

The discovery of meaning in suffering is, remarkably enough, never a purely individual undertaking. The word of Christ, ''Where two or three are gathered in my name, there I am in their midst,'' is never so applicable as here. People are called to com-passion with each other. When they are solitary, they seldom discover the meaning of what is happening to them.

People must not only break bread with each other, but also share suffering. Human suffering is a puzzle whose separate pieces, meaningless in themselves, begin to form an image only when they are put together. That image becomes completely clear only when the pieces of our own times as well as elements from Scripture and Tradition are taken into the construction of the ultimate meaning.

That is why it is important to listen to the various, sometimes divergent, answers that believers have found to the enigma of suffering up to now. It is striking that all these answers are basically variations on the same theme, albeit in the most diverse keys and on the most diverse instruments.

Psychology and the Question of Meaning

The Jewish psychiatrist Victor Frankl, who survived terrible years of concentration camp, calls people, not "pleasure-seekers" or "success-seekers," as did Freud and Adler, but rather "meaning-seekers." Today, people are frustrated not so much for want of sexuality or of appreciation, but for want of meaning.

The question "Why are we alive?" is doubtless as old as the human phenomenon itself. What is new is the fact that more and more modern prophets have no response to this question. What is worse, they explain that this primordial question is insoluble in principle. Camus said, "I am afraid that there simply is no answer."

In his work *Man's Search for Meaning*, Frankl tells us that most of his patients, having found no answer to the aforementioned question, had become sick or depressed. Though it is not the task of the psychiatrist to formulate this answer, he affirmed that an answer does exist, for giving meaning is not a psychological but a religious matter. In other words, it is more the work of ministry than of medicines or social works.

"Naturally, a psychiatrist cannot tell a patient what this meaning is, but in any case, he can let it be seen that life *does have* meaning, that this meaning is present for everyone, and moreover, that life itself preserves its meaning in all circumstances . . . to the last glimpse, to the last breath" (V. Frankl, *The Unheard Cry for Meaning* [New York, 1978] 31).

In *The Unconscious God*, Frankl goes on to explain why the question of meaning is insoluble for so many: modern people have lost their sense of God. It is not sexuality which has become repressed, but rather God. Frankl notes that his patients were "immediately prepared to speak of their sex lives to the most intimate, even perverse, detail, but that as soon as their intimate religious life gets mentioned, the same patients immediately display inhibitions" (V. Frankl, *Der unbewusste Gott. Psychotherapie und Religion* [Munich, 1977] 43).

Suffering is a phase of life in which the question about the meaning of life is generally felt much more acutely than during periods of success and euphoria. Frankl, in *A Psychiatrist Survives the Concentration Camp*, testifies that many of his fellow prisoners in this hell discovered God and hence remained alive, while others were so radically shaken that not only did all their faith disappear, but also their will to live. Elie Wiesel, another Jewish survivor of Auschwitz, wrote of one of his friends, "As soon as he became aware of the first crack in his faith, he lost all motive for struggling on, and began to die," and of another who shared the same fate, "Poor Akiba! If only he could have gone on believing in God, if only he could have discovered a sign of God on Mount Calvary, he would not have fallen away" (E. Wiesel, *Night* [London, 1960] 77, 88).

Modern psychiatry points out that people become depressed and miserable when what is happening to them seems meaningless. Is religion then nothing more than a deceptive means to desensitize the pain of this meaninglessness, or at least to make it bearable? Only pieces of cloth that really exist can be used to make an effective patch. Faith convictions can seem useful for various things, or even be misused, but in both cases what is necessary is a faith that is already existing. This is something that many functionalists do not see. We can use a branch as a walking stick, or even as a rod to strike a child. But the existence of walking sticks or of old-fashioned teachers does not explain why new branches keep growing on a healthy tree, any more than the existence of religious functions (and even misuse of them) can explain why people believe in God.

It is typical for people today that, because of the decline of their awareness of God, they are on the look-out for something purely human or psychological to give meaning to suffering and death. The overwhelming international success of two best-sellers, Gray's *Le Livre de la vie: pour trouver le bonheur, le courage, et l'espoir* and H. Kushner's *When Bad Things Happen to Good People*, is an indication of this. The first is a pagan book, the second a liberal-Jewish one; both works are also taken up, quoted, and propagated by a number of Christians. Both agree that, in their suffering, people must not reach for God as an "emergency-brake," since this God, if God exists, is not very efficient. People have to help themselves. The latter author, a rabbi, does not hesitate to write, "The primary goal of religion . . . is not to bring people into contact with God, but with each other." To put it more bluntly, religion is not a question of prayer, but of fluid, beneficial contacts and smooth social relationships. Here, religion becomes a sort of psychological first-aid station.

L. Kolakowski understood that faith must be much more than a psychological analgesic when he wrote, in crass but plain words: "Religion is the manner in which people accept their lives as an inevitable defeat" (*Kan de Duivel Verlost Worden?*, 114). This means that sooner or later every thinking, down-to-earth person realizes that life brings with it great disillusionments and exits onto an inevitable death. The fact that, in spite of this, people persevere and can even be happy (even though it used to be easier than now; note the present-day number of depressions and suicides) indicates that for these people there must be something "sacral" or "eternal" that gives meaning to everything.

Psychology has never really had the pretension of being a "meaning-giver." It wisely leaves that role to philosophy and religion. But in our day, a growing number of philosophers (as, for example, Sartre and Camus) and even theologians (such as Kushner) do not recognize any meaning at all in suffering and failure, and only pose the question of psychological survival. The meaning-question is replaced by the more pragmatic question: how do I work through this suffering without psychologically submitting to it? To put it more bluntly: how do I push everything painful into oblivion and succeed in remaining optimistic in spite of everything? We can never be grateful enough to these crucial thinkers for their house-cleaning work in the old bazaar of pious platitudes, cheap solutions, empty phrases of consolation, and psycho-religious expedients. On the other hand, repressing the question of meaning to the unconscious does not solve anything; according to psychiatrists such as Frankl, Van den Berg, or Görres, the refusal (or the inability) to take up this question is the foremost cause of the pessimistic malaise that so strikingly characterizes modern people.

Christianity's Answer to Tragedy

When tragedy is defined as "a drama with a disastrous ending," and the tragic as "the painful consciousness that a blind fate determines human life," then a Christian vision of life can never be called tragic. Christendom and tragedy are mutually exclusive, according to the Jewish atheist G. Steiner in his book *The Death of Tragedy*. According to him, Judaeo-Christian thought has put an end to the possibilities of creating genuine tragedies any more. It is hard to call the tragedies of Shakespeare, Schiller, or even Ibsen "tragedies" in the strict sense. These dramatists are too Christian for that. No matter what disasters may overtake people, Christians discover a providential God behind them. According to Steiner, Christianity is an anti-tragic vision of life. For believers, a "Christian tragedy" is a contradiction in terms. Those who use concepts such as heaven, Providence, or divine justice and goodness are simultaneously making the sign of the cross over blind chance and meaningless misery. Meaninglessness is the only tragedy, and therefore incomprehensible.

Perhaps we might say that tragedy is celebrating its discreet return to the Western stage, not in heavy and sad drama, but in the bitter morality plays which are critical of their own times, films and events that are impervious to any sort of transcendence and faith. Perhaps Bergman's *Scenes from a Marriage*, Albee's *Who's Afraid of Virginia Woolf?*, or Miller's *Death of a Salesman* are much more tragic than Goethe's *Faust* or Chekhov's *Three Sisters*, for the world of the former remains hermetically sealed against everything that could transcend human suffering. That is why the atmosphere of these little worlds is so oppressively tragic.

The only *Weltanschauung* that is just as anti-tragic as Christianity is Marxism. For Marx, too, suffering and misery do have a temporal meaning. The Marxist hopes in a "classless society" from which all suffering will have disappeared. This earthly paradise gives meaning to the most radical sacrifice, the most painful methods, and the most awful deprivations, at least as long as they appear necessary for social revolution and progress. Remember the slogan of May 1968: "A revolution that requires sacrifice is a revolution *à la Papa*." Well, the Marxism of Papa Marx does indeed ask for sacrifices. That is why in 1968 some wanted to look for more moderate, less costly scenarios of revolutionary commitment. Those (such as Marx) who speak of sacrifice speak also of sacrifice that is "meaningful."

Real tragedy is never a question of painful problems that can be solved by scientific progress, revolution, or any sort of noble commitment, but of an unavoidable movement toward destruction and death against which we humans stand powerless. It is hardly to the point if we call this blind and unjust fate an "accident" (as does the modern atheist Monod), or "Moira" or the "Fates" (as did the Greeks) or *Schicksal* (as did Goethe and Schiller). What is important is the fact that the tragic person suspects the existence of a meaningless, unjust, and incalculable force at work behind everything that happens and is still happening, a force that is always criss-crossing the lives of well-meaning, even heroic, people, and that always makes their final end a disaster.

For G. Steiner, the core of the biblical message lies in the conviction that the course of events—as much in the evolution of the cosmos in general as in an individual's life in particular—is never blind and accidental, not even in its most painful periods.

The most depressing aspect of human suffering, according to Simone Weil, is the fact that God often disguises the evil that touches us as a "blind mechanism." In other words, God hides behind the appearances of accidents precisely when we need God the most. But God hides only to make the joy of personal discovery possible for us. In the following chapter, we intend to trace how and where Christians have found God in the night of their suffering, and especially what salutary meaning they have come to perceive behind this suffering.

CHAPTER EIGHT

The Cross: A Process of Expropriation

Christ's Presence in Suffering

Those who wonder how a true Christian experiences suffering would do better to consult the mystics or masters of the spiritual life than average believers. Would not a lecturer on Flemish baroque painting do better to use slides of Peter Paul Rubens' works rather than reproductions of mediocre painters from his period (who nevertheless are much more plentiful and statistically more representative)? Art history is not concerned with average robot-photos but with unique, successful models which were normative and set the tone for their times. Spirituality, too, is not interested in researching the social "average" with respect to faith; rather it seeks to be enlightened by great figures in whom the best things of their times came to spiritual fruition.

First of all, it is striking that all the Christian mystics bring suffering into explicit relationship with the crucified Christ. In other words, for them, the cross is as central as the crucifix that traditionally has a place of honor in the living room of the Christian family. For them, suffering remains an insoluble problem, a stumbling block, or a scandal, if it is not seen against the background of Calvary. For the mystics, Christ's cross is not a pious extra or a classical symbol that we can add to other interesting and common human considerations of suffering. It is not a new variation on a primitive, archetypal human theme. With Christ, humanity received a whole new vision of suffering. Yet Christ is far more than a new "meaning-giver." Most of all, he is an efficacious power and help for the suffering person.

A priest face to face with the suffering of a broken marriage or an incurable illness knows two ways to handle the dilemma: either he involves the person of Christ himself (however difficult this may be in our days) or he confines himself to a few heart-felt words of sympathy. If no mention is made of Christ, sooner or later, everything remains at the level of a psychological approach.

Wittgenstein once said, ''To believe in God means to come to the insight that, in spite of everything, life does have a meaning.'' Einstein expressed the same thing in a different way when he wrote, ''To have found an answer to the question of the meaning of life means to have become a believer.'' What meaning, then, did the Christian mystics discover in the suffering that came to them? Did they find life really meaningful even in their darkest and most confused moments? Did they believe in God even when God seemed to strike them with the rod of fate?

If we state that the great Christians always situate suffering in the context of Christ's cross, it does not mean that they viewed the passion narrative as a means of solving crises or questions of meaning. Because their whole life lies imbedded in God, their suffering also appears to find a place on this religious canvas. No matter how frightened they sometimes become when the storm-wind arises on the lake of their lives, they never lose sight of the sleeping Christ.

Submitting to the Hand of God

That which most characterizes true Christians is their steady search for the will of God. In other words: in every situation, Christians let themselves be led by their awareness of ''vocation.'' In contrast to Buddhists or pantheists, Christians do not believe that it is their ultimate destiny to be absorbed by God or to be assumed into the All. Rather, God calls us to an eternal love-relationship. In this steadily growing friendship, mystics experience that God gradually takes over the helm. God becomes the only guide. ''Ordinary'' believers know and believe this in their best moments, but they do not experience it in a sensible way, as mystics do. God becomes the true center of their lives. The same pattern is seen when people fall in love; their attention as well as their feelings are now concentrated steadily on the partner. When people are seized by a strongly felt love for God, they experience that God begins to "expropriate" them. Concretely, this means that the loving or religious person no longer holds back any "private possession" to which God is refused access. There is no longer anything of which the mystic says: "This is *my* affair; You keep out of it!"

This certainly does not mean that mystics no longer have their own identity. "All identities necessarily have an other with whom they enter into relationship; by this relationship my own self-identity comes into existence" (R. Laing, *Self and Others*, [London, 1969] 66). A mother is only mother through her child. A person is only fully human and fully faith-filled through God. People become wholly themselves only through those to whom they fully give themselves and (thus *if* they give themselves to someone; this self-gift can be refused, which unfortunately is not rare).

Mystics feel deeply that God draws them to Godself. God expropriates them, though they can always refuse that, too. The great discovery of all mystics is that this process of expropriation never goes on without pain and misery. More precisely, they discover that all suffering means a further step in their expropriation-process or identity-formation. Suffering brings a person closer to communion or union with God. God never takes away something from a person unless God plans to give something more essential in its place (although this "essential something" is seldom directly experienced as such).

Like the cutting hand of the healing surgeon, God's work is ultimately always positive, no matter how incomprehensible and painful. Do patients need to understand directly the "why" of every surgical precaution or operation? Yet surgeons can make mistakes—divine Providence never. This expropriation-process goes on consciously

among the mystics. At certain moments, they realize what
is going on in them: it is God who is busy with them and
who is creating space for a more intimate dwelling. At
other moments, it seems as if God is absent and has left
them in the lurch. Think, for example, of Christ's own
prayerful sigh, "My God, my God, why hast Thou forsaken me?" or of John of the Cross' "night of the soul."

Ordinary believers (not to mention unbelievers), live all
of this with less awareness. They try to believe that their
suffering is not meaningless, and that God is always concerned with people. But most do not feel it. That is why it
is helpful in moments of pain and dismay to seek counsel
from those who know more about it, namely, mystics and
gifted people. As a Jewish rabbi once said, "Some people
are God's language." It is especially in the case of mystics
that this seems to be true. Every person is made to love
and to be loved, just as every person (and not just the
gifted) is made to believe in and to be inhabited by God.
Yet just as we find solitary people (i.e., without human
relationships) in this world, so too there are people who
have no idea of God whatsoever. By a painful scouring
process, God takes more and more possession of the
human soul. Only the true believer has any notion of
what is going on at such times. Unbelievers and rebels
meanwhile experience only meaningless suffering.

It often happens that, in times of success and resultant
self-confidence, God strikes a person's property. God
often enough interrupts human enterprise and busyness.
This sometimes leads to the misconception that God
begrudges human happiness. The typical pagan expression
(which even finds a place on Christian tongues) "Knock
on wood" testifies to this. It refers to a magic ritual by
which people grasped the wooden altar as a testimonial
that they would be glad to offer even the best portion of
their belongings if only the gods would leave them alone
in periods of success and euphoria, as if the gods were
jealous of human happiness, and would often strike if
people were too prosperous.

What is false here is the idea that God would interfere
with human happiness and even punish out of envy. Here

it is not so much a question of divine jealousy as of divine vengeance. We hear the statement that successful people often show a tendency to lose their sense of religious reality and *therefore* they are sometimes "touched" by God in their possessions. But in the Christian perspective, there is no question of interpreting this as "punishment" or "vengeance"; rather misfortune can serve as a reminder of reality.

Napoleon arrogantly said, "There is no such thing as suffering defeat; there are only stupid people side by side with intelligent ones." Only a naïve person speaks like this, someone who has not yet become acquainted with the shock of suffering. It often happens that people who have become this obtuse in their self-conceit are shaken awake by God as by a sudden change of tide or an unexpected turn of the wind.

God is the great Intruder into human life. The gateway by which God seeks entrance to the human heart is the creaking door of suffering. "We are, as it were, plants, and have only one choice: to expose ourselves to the Light or not," writes Simone Weil.

When God begins to open the door of Light, people can still hide behind the curtain of rebellious refusal. But God never enters where God is considered unwelcome. Sooner or later, however, the self-deception of successful people is providentially interrupted. For some, this is when the door is flung open. Others, however, rebelliously resist their lot and refuse to take a look at what is really happening to them.

To consider suffering as a process of union with God (that is to say, as an expropriation process drawing us out of solitary self-enclosure) means two things at once: that God suffers in us, and that God is present in a special way in all those who suffer. In other words, when I suffer, God is present in me in a special way; and people in need are, as it were, a tabernacle in which God dwells in an eminent way.

As Paul says, "To know Christ means becoming aware of our communion with His passion" and "becoming like Him in His death" (cf. Phil 3:10). By "knowledge of

Christ,'' Paul does not mean having theological concepts, but knowing ourselves as existentially bound to him (as for example a young man knows his fiancée). In a certain perspective, it is true that misfortune never comes alone. It always comes accompanied by God. Christian mystics never hesitate to recognize God's healing hand in every pain that touches them, except for pain that they consciously cause themselves, for self-torture is masochism. No matter how closely suffering can bring us to God, suffering that is artifically created is never a way to reach God. The English mystic Benedict of Canfield writes, ''Therefore our own pains—insofar as they are not ours but those of Christ—must be deeply respected. How wonderful! And more: our pains are as much to be revered as those of Jesus Christ in His own passion. For if people correctly adore Him with so much devotion in images on the Good Friday cross, why may we not then revere Him on the living cross that we ourselves are?''

The mystics, then, never hesitate to consider their own sufferings as a precious treasure, for that suffering is the shrine in which they bear God in themselves: ''The perfect see God in all things, but all the more in the sufferings . . . in which He is present in such an exceptional way'' (Benedict of Canfield, *Over de Navolging van Jezus in de Mystische Beleving*, ed. P. Mommaers [Bonheiden, 1980] 53).

Believers are never expropriated automatically. We are naturally averse to every form of intrusion and dismantling. By nature we are defensive and egocentric. Something in us offers resistance to God. That something is what we call ''original sin.''

Being Freed for the Other

God has created and intended us to be ex-centric beings: we are not created for self-fulfillment alone, but for love. Our ultimate destiny lies not in an independent or undisciplined self, but in the arms of the Beloved. For we are created "according to God's image," that is to say, in order to love and be loved, or, to give and to receive. We are created to experience our self and our possessions "in community." In order to do that, more is necessary than letting our instinctive impulses run their free course, for we have a double tendency within us. On the one hand, we have an insatiable desire for self-preservation, self-expansion, and ownership. Indeed, the ego experiences itself as the natural center of the world, a center that will inevitably come into collision with other would-be centers (perhaps even with the real Center of all reality: the "Omega Point"). On the other hand, the ego wants an other to be the pole of attraction and the center of its life. More simply put: even the most autonomous and self-willed people long once in a while for love and liberation from their own (self-made) solitude. Self-preservation and self-surrender are a two-pronged, and sometimes conflicting, desire in every person. An introverted, quiet, or fearful person feels a stronger need for privacy, self-recollection, and independence. The extroverted character, on the other hand, cannot get along without contacts, relationships, and continual expression of what is going on inside. Even the most autistic person, however, hungers to be freed from the stronghold of self-enclosure, while even the most superficial person feels the need of a moment of inward reflection now and again.

The first step toward the other always implies a giving up of something of oneself. A relationship presupposes a certain measure of "spiritual strip-tease" (and in marriage, even more than that!). Therefore, the other who comes to me is often experienced as an intruder against whom I want protection. But the greatest intruder is God, who "tries the heart and the mind" (Jer 20:12), and who calls us away out of our familiar selves as he called Abraham away from his "land, tribe, and family," and the apostles away from their nets and fishing boats. Only in the light of faith will we realize that, though separation always brings suffering with it, every exodus can be the first step toward the "promised land."

The tendency to ownership, as well as the desire for openness and relationship, are in themselves healthy, divinely-created powers. But the first is no more than a necessary condition for making the second step possible. Those who have no inner riches have nothing to offer others. A liberating word can be born only where there is silence. Unfortunately, the order is sometimes reversed: others are considered as objects with which people try to adorn their own lives. They use relationships in order to enhance their self-importance. Even God and prayer get used in order to give more flavor to their own devotional life.

The ego sometimes seeks cheaper means than true love to escape self-enclosure. Alcohol, drugs, rhythmic music, emotional trances, political ecstasies, demagogic euphoria, and other more exotic forms of "consciousness expansion" are only a few variants out of the rich gamut of artificial techniques by which people try to get "out of themselves," to breathe in a more relaxing atmosphere. The real vacating of the possessive ego can succeed only by way of the bridge of faithful relationship. Rescue from the security of the prison-cell of one's own self takes place—as in every birth—mostly in pain. The first role that suffering can play is the breaking open of the defensive bulwark in which we are continually shutting ourselves up. But this suffering cannot be used like a master key that works on every little door. The cross comes most often when one least expects it. It is God—and the life circumstances allowed by God—that liberate us again and again, just as God freed Peter from prison. Peter at first thought he was dreaming. It was only later that the reality of what happened struck him: "Now I am sure that the Lord has sent his angel and rescued me" (Acts 12:11).

Belief in Providence means discerning the hand of God even in the painful things that happen to us. It is always a hand that frees us from the prison of our ego, a hand that expropriates in order to make possible a common possession of love. In 1954, Hammarskjöld noted in his diary: "Then only did I see that the wall had never really existed, and that the unheard-of is now already here."

Thus, in suffering, the mystic experiences that God was already present in everyone from the very beginning. What is new is only this: that God gradually begins to dismantle the barricades behind which people thought they were safely hidden from unwanted intruders.

If God comes "as a thief in the night," it is never to steal or to rob, but in order to make an exchange, to heal, and to ennoble. In short, God comes to initiate the process of divinization to which every person is called. "If you want to become everything that you are ultimately capable of," writes Hadewijch in her second letter, "then become what He is." That total self-surrender to God here on earth means, in Christian terms, "to have fellowship with His Son" (1 Cor 1:9) even when this Son has borne a cross and died on that cross. But the believer knows that Good Friday is the last valley or the ultimate vale of tears on the way to the mountain-top of the final resurrection.

The process of expropriation is really the struggle between what A. Chouraqui has called "the little and the big ego." Only if people dare to break through and give up the petty enclosure of their "precious ego" do they become themselves and come out into the greatness of the divine life to which they are called. Their personality (or ego) becomes greater the more they dare to open the door to the Other. But when this does not happen, God often breaks down the human wall of defense.

CHAPTER NINE

Suffering: Purgatory on Earth

Purifying Our Natures

From time to time we hear it said that some people have already had their purgatory on earth. In reality, however, everyone lives through a *purgatorium* on earth. They experience a quantum of suffering that has a purifying effect. In addition to the already-mentioned function of expropriation, suffering also plays a purificatory role. What precisely needs to get purified? The answer is simple: our taste or sense for what is essential. Ruusbroec puts it this way: "If a person takes pleasure from other things, then he will never be able to savor what God is" (J. van Ruusbroec, *Werken*, vol. 1, 217).

As long as children are absorbed heart and soul in their play, they take no thought or interest in their homework. It often happens that a mother takes away sweets from her children so they do not spoil their appetite for supper. Sometimes God takes away from us valuable things of lesser importance so that we will gradually pay more attention and get a feel for the things of God. Just as children who walk around an amusement park and stop by the first attraction often have to be told by their father to go further, as "there is still a lot more to see," so also people are often withdrawn by God from what has preoccupied them too much. For life has ever so much more to offer than the tinsel to which we are occasionally so firmly attached and with which we like to play. People are often so busy with transitory things that they have no notion of what is of lasting value. "We sometimes think that

our natural life-milieu is a grey, neutral world. But that
sort of world and this state of affairs are transitory. In reality, we are standing on the threshhold of a wholly new
world. Someone ought to make us see this and accept it,''
writes H. Miller (H. Miller, *Plexus*, [New York, 1965] 88).

Now, this ''someone'' is God. By apparently accidental,
sometimes very painful, life-circumstances, our attention is
fixed on what awaits us on the other side of the threshold
of the transitory. In fact, suffering always destroys something in us, but only in order to put something else in its
place that does *not* come from us.

That which has to be purified in us by suffering is the
world of our desires and the whole arsenal of our so-called
spontaneous or natural needs. These latter can reign supreme in us, to the extent that our deepest desires and
true hunger are not even noticeable.

According to Ruusbroec, people differ one from another
with respect to their ''hunger.'' Modern psychologists
would perhaps prefer to speak of lust-objects or desires.
That for which a person most hungers and thirsts with all
his strength at once determines what this person is worth
and that typifies him. But ''religiously-inclined'' people or
''religious temperaments'' do not exist. All people bear
within themselves a desire for God, even though this desire can become as repressed as the desire for sexual life
was among Puritans. Desire for God is a little plant that
grows very gradually and is easily choked out by the wild
flora of insignificant weeds. Therefore, suffering also has a
''weeding-out'' function.

Maturation and true humanism have to do with the
building up of a true hierarchy of values. Sooner or later,
the young will let their toys fall from their hands in order
to grasp for things that give more satisfaction. But when
people make an idol of trash, or if their ''darling'' is their
hunting dog, the shock of a loss can mean the first step
toward a more humane awareness. Sometimes only
bankruptcy of what is of secondary importance leads
people to seek for what is genuine. In other words, in
order for them to savor what is genuine, what is *not* genu-

ine must first be removed from their mouths. When this latter does not happen, God often providentially intervenes. Yet we are not talking about an anthropomorphic exchange or trade-off of objects. Simone Weil sees the meaning of suffering in that "a person at the end of his rope, in spite of his many potentialities, will finally stretch out his hand, stand still, look and wait." Only then can the silence of God's goodness really touch this person. Only then is this person ready to listen to the word of God. It is in this context that a person can understand the difficult saying of Christ: "Woe to you, rich!" Here it is not a question of taking a social position against the financially strong and for the proletarians, in a Marxist class-struggle frame of reference. Here, Christ is warning the rich of the fact that the poor have *one* great advantage over them, namely, that the poor never have their hands full. Their hands are free. By nature, they reach their hands out for help, support, and rescue.

But the rich have the tendency to clasp their supposed treasures tightly and snugly in their hands, even if these riches often, in the long run, turn out to be tinsel or toys. This is why sometimes a person is providentially stricken with poverty (in talents, health, success, longer life expectancy, etc.). Where there is no neediness, no rescuing or liberating hand is clasped, not even the hand of God. Where there is no hunger, no nourishing bread is eaten. Those who do not feel ill never consult a doctor. "Those who are well have no need of a physician, but those who are sick. I came not to call the righteous, but sinners" (Mark 2:17). This is how the Lord expounded his warning word addressed to the "rich."

In other words, if the "ten lepers" had not been afflicted, perhaps they would never have dared take the step to really meet Christ. Christ did not come in order to make possible an alternative or supernatural cure of lepers. But leprosy made possible a personal meeting with Christ. If he had not been conscious of his moral guilt and his deceptive practices, Zacchaeus perhaps would never have had the joy of being able to receive Jesus under his roof.

Suffering can be the first step toward turning to what is
essential. The euphoria of success, however, makes a person forgetful and even insensitive.

A New Orientation

Those who look attentively at an object without manag-
ing to discover precisely what it is change position in
order to get a better view. Now, suffering almost always
"moves" a person. It gives one a new standpoint or a
new look on things that previously seemed unclear or un-
sightly or that one never even noticed.

People growing old learn to look with new eyes at
things that have long been familiar to them. Nothing shar-
pens and purifies our look at people and things as much
as the shock of suffering. Tinsel fades, the atmosphere
falls away, and flattery dies away. When the time of need
comes, only true friends remain. Prayer becomes real or
else it dies out in rebellious embitterment.

The Trappist abbot and psychiatrist J. E. Bamberger of
Genesee describes the monastic vocation as follows: "The
monk refuses to go along with the existing system and its
values. He has his own priorities and ideals. His withdrawal and detachment always aim at creating a new life-
center" (J. E. Bamberger, "Defining the Center. A Monastic Point of View," in *Cistercian Studies* [1980] 384). A person's life-center, or focus of all attention and interest, can
be career, success, money, fame, relationships, etc. According to Bamberger, what the monk does from an inner
call (going in search of the *true* center of life) is what many
must do by necessity when an apparently terminal suffering suddenly comes upon them. People who had directed
their lives toward a secondary or unimportant center often
feel shaken by the shock of an unexpected grief. They get
disoriented. The world's compass that till then had guided
them with a steadiness that had come to appear normal
goes awry. In such moments of crisis, God calls us to a
rectification of our course.

The people or things that we lose in suffering are not necessarily inferior or bad. But in the long run, they must never be the center of our life or the axis around which everything smoothly turns. God wants to be that center and axis, even though it is left to each person to agree to this or not. But God never places us before the dilemma, "Either Me or the world." This world (and all that is beautiful in it) is a creation and a gift of God, of which "God saw that it was good." It is a question of priority in choice, not of exclusivity in love.

In his book *August '14*, Solzhenitsyn writes, "There is something much more fundamental and important than social order, namely inward order . . . . In it is our primary vocation: to put our inward order in place." By "inward order," the Nobel laureate means a right hierarchy of values and attachments for which one is ready to give everything. With one person it is her child; with another, it is the family honor or a career; for a third it is his priestly apostolate or mission work, etc. For these people, everything stands or falls with their item of top priority. If they fail, then it seems to them that life no longer has any meaning. Now, no matter how valuable and irreplaceable these various treasures may be, they are still transitory as long as God is not the center of one's life. The shock of suffering is always an invitation to a new orientation.

In the Book of Job, the Hebrew Scriptures' great "treatise on suffering," Job does sit in sackcloth and ashes, but he certainly does not disdain creation and its beauty. Through his suffering, rather, he comes to a new worldview. He comes to a "re-orientation" of his life, in the etymological meaning of the word. He discovers where the true orient lies, whence the enduring Light shall rise, a Light that will give new and lasting shape to everything that was previously taken away from him. The most important discovery at the end of his process of apparent disintegration is an insight of a religious nature: "I had heard of thee by the hearing of the ear, but now my eye sees thee." So runs the final verse of this Jewish book.

With this word, Job's long argumentative complaint has evolved into a deep prayer. A bitter monologue in which he challenges God comes to an end in silent dialogue. The process is always the same: God makes his way to the human heart by first of all emptying and purifying that heart.

Transformation into God's People

The beautiful and the somber things that life brings for every person greatly resemble the incomprehensible pieces of a puzzle. Some pieces fascinate and attract us. Others we would rather not look at. The model by which all the pieces, good as well as evil, ultimately fit into each other and make up a unity is the slowly emerging *Gestalt* of our vocation. This vocation is not a programmed course that astrologers, for instance, can discover as if our divinely planned way already stands written in the stars. It is also not a general model such as we often find on the top of the puzzle-box. Rather, it is an image that only becomes clear little by little by humbly comparing and testing our deficiencies, talents, defeats, possibilities, or weaknesses and strengths. It is an image that always has to do with the Christian way of life as it stands sketched out in the many stories of the gospel.

"If people knew that God suffers with us, and even much more than we do, because of all the evil and sorrow on earth, then perhaps many things would change, and many people would feel relieved and liberated," writes J. Maritain (cited in F. Varillon, *La Souffrance de Dieu*, 14). The greatest pain of a mother who brings her little baby to the hospital for an operation probably consists in the fact that she can by no means explain to her infant why the coming pain is necessary and beneficial. God knows that no one is ever going to be able to understand fully his or her portion of suffering in the world or even be able to perceive clearly its ultimate meaning. The reason for this is not God's impotence, but the finitude of humans. This

lack of understanding and perception is itself the main
point of all human suffering. Related to this, Hadewych,
in her second letter, very correctly notes: ''All misery that
people bear willingly on account of God is well-pleasing to
God and brings us near to God. But if we knew how
much God is pleased by it, then it would no longer be
misery for us.'' The point is evidently not that God takes
sadistic pleasure in our pain, but rather that God finds
pleasure in the fact that people continue to believe, in
spite of their pain and their head-shaking incomprehen-
sion as to why all this is necessary at all. So also a mother
counts herself happy if she notices that her child does not
go into panic because he knows and feels his mother is
present near him.

Suffering brings us to the bridge of faith, but it does not
at the same time put us on the sunny side of certainty and
evidence. Suffering points to the way of faith—a long way
that we can either take up or refuse. Suffering never
works as an automatic electric switch that can cast light on
human problems in one flip. Rather, suffering is a journey
of discovery in the dark. Only those who look carefully
see after a while a light that offers a way out. This light is
always of a religious nature.

Perhaps we can summarize the core of the Christian
message as follows: in the person of Jesus Christ, it becomes clear for us not only who God really is, but also
what it means to be really human. Moreover, it is revealed
to us in the crucified Christ (and this insight even seems
to be of central importance) that religion and suffering
have much to do with each other. Suffering is more than
an accidental blot on an otherwise glorious and problem-
free relationship between God and ourselves. Suffering
confronts each of us in a special way with God.

Teilhard de Chardin calls human pain a ''sacrament of
transformation,'' that is to say, a force that changes us.
What gets transformed by suffering is our human ''taste,''
that is, the direction or the object of our desires. Suffering
awakens new and deeper sensations, while old attractions
lose their strength. Suffering criss-crosses our original plan

of life and forces us either to re-examine our first project or else to give up all further projects in despair. Yet suffering never operates as an infallible, automatic transformer. It always places us before a choice.

"In order to penetrate us in a definitive way, God must dig in us, empty us, and win a place for Godself," says Teilhard. "God has to rework us, recast and rearrange the molecules of our whole being. The great triumph of the Creator and Redeemer is found in the fact that He has changed a principle of universal destruction and deterioration into a factor of essential revival" (P. Teilhard de Chardin, *Sur la souffrance* [Paris, 1974] 84–85).

We might say that God has not "changed" this principle but has used it since the beginning of the ages. God makes positive use of the negative principle of suffering, because the latter appears to be an especially efficacious spiritual force. No other principle so strongly guarantees the growth of human love, creativity, and freedom on the one hand, and the expropriation or liberation of those wrapped up in themselves on the other. Above all, suffering creates an increasing taste for the things of heaven.

"The exceptional greatness of Christianity lies in the fact that it offers no supernatural remedy *against* suffering, but rather a supernatural use of suffering," said Simone Weil (S. Weil, *La Pesanteur et la Grace*, 86).

CHAPTER TEN

Prayer of Petition:
What It Means and Doesn't Mean

The Need for Petition

When one is stricken with disaster or illness, does it make sense to call on God for help or to pray for healing? Would God then be letting possible intervention depend on a human prayer of petition? What is more, does God ever "intervene" in the natural course of things which he himself created and has willed as such? Many such questions surround the difficult problem of the meaning of petitionary prayer.

Two things are clear right from the start. First, there is no doubt that Christ himself repeatedly praised petitionary prayer and more than once prayed to the Father for the needs of others, as well as for himself. Second, every spiritual writer has always stressed that petitionary prayer is not the noblest or most perfect form of prayer. In other words, true prayer should not limit itself to petitions and requests.

In human psychology, the act of making a request is important. Mothers teach their children not to demand and grab things they want, but to ask for them instead. Even when they clearly intend to give their children what they need or want, good parents still expect a polite and express request. Family life is not a question of silent give and take, but above all, of living and speaking with one another. These are two elements that children have to learn even though there are more noble forms of dialogue imaginable than, "May I have another piece of chocolate?" or "May I go play now?" Dialogue is what transforms

human beings into persons. Language is what creates
them, and not the reverse: people did not invent language
at a given moment along with the bow and arrow. Creatures with no notion of a language are infra-human beings. Only when language comes about does the human
being arrive on stage.

The Prussian King Frederich, according to one story, let
two healthy nurslings be isolated and well cared for, except that they were never to hear a single word spoken.
He wanted to be able to see for himself what "natural language" these children would speak after a few years had
elapsed. The result will not surprise any psychologist or
teacher: the children died before they were two years old.
Children need warmth and good care more than milk.
Children need physical and psychological contact; that is,
they need bodily and mental communication. The same
goes for humans with respect to God. People not only
converse with each other; they also reflect by themselves,
and now and then they even address themselves to God.
Conversation, reflection, and prayer are fundamental re-
quirements of a well-balanced person. When even one of
these three factors is lacking, something dies in a person.
She or he becomes autistic, superficial, or materialistic.

For a child, the first occasion for speaking or even crying
and shouting is an acute feeling of discomfort. The child
"misses" something and so "asks" for that thing,
whether it be with gestures, screams, words that have
been learned, or later with personally constructed sen-
tences. The child needs all sorts of things. Naturally, his
mother knows this best of all. Still, often enough she will
wait for an express request from the child. The child's discomfort or need fills an important role: it forces him to go
out of himself and speak. With respect to prayer also, the
situation of need has an important function. Need forms
an occasion for seeking contact with God. Need teaches a
person to pray. That is why Paul calls our weakness our
greatest riches. Prayer is not meant to get rid of human
weaknesses or illnesses. Rather, the reverse is true: because they feel weak, threatened, or helpless, those who

suffer almost naturally call on God for help. The most
primitive, but still indispensable, form of prayer is the insistent, almost spontaneous prayer of petition. It is a form
of prayer that never becomes entirely superfluous. To their
request: "Lord, teach us to pray!" the Lord impressed on
the heart of his apostles the need to ask the Father again
and again, "Give us this day our daily bread!" At that
moment, the Lord was counseling them to ask God for
certain concrete things.

No matter what children might ask, their mother is sure
of two things. The first is that children are insatiable. If
she gives them everything they ask, they will certainly become spoiled and unhappy. Second, children do not know
as well as their mother what they really need most. There
are things that no good, far-seeing mother will ever give
or allow her children, just because she loves them too
much to give them those things. But in the meantime, the
mother is happy that the children even ask. In mature asking and answering, contact and intimacy increase between
mother and children. Mother knows—and she is really
proud and happy about it—that her children ask things of
her that they would never dare ask of their father or their
teacher. Nothing is more painful for a mother than to realize that the growing children think they no longer need
her. When children no longer ask for anything, the mother
soon feels superfluous. Something analogous is also true
for the relationship between God and human beings.

Everyone knows that we are speaking anthropomorphi-
cally here. But does not Christ in the Gospels continually
speak in human terms and parables about God? Is the
Bible anything but a human way of speaking about God
and a divine way of speaking about humanity? In other
words, the Bible is an anthropomorphic theology and an
anthropology that begins with the revealed principle that
humanity is created according to God's own image. (Those
who see humanity in this light also learn to know something about God in the process.)

As a result of need, the helpless person—and very spe-
cially, the child—learns to pray. Later, this person will

learn through experience that neediness and misery, far more than success and accomplishments, are what inspire people to travel to Lourdes or make a retreat or plan time for reflection. Suffering and need always alter a person's relationship to God. Children can go play outside all day, but when they hurt themselves, they immediately come running in tears to their mother, who seems practically to have been forgotten—and perhaps really was. In need, a person turns back to God and learns to pray.

It is surely painful for a mother that she cannot always make it plain to her children why *this* cannot be and why *that* must be. The children's capacity for understanding is still too small for such information. "Later" they will understand everything. Not a single human prayer goes unheard. Just like a good mother, God knows better and God also gives something better. The children's need and the mother's real love are the two poles between which their relationship comes into being. The depth of the mother-child relationship is defined by the child's need and the mother's selflessness. It is well known that parents have remarkable love for their handicapped child. The Lord too repeats again and again, "It is not the healthy who need a doctor but the sick." The old rabbinic saying, "The cow desires to give suck far more than the little calf wants to suckle" can be translated into religious terminology: "God desires to give far more than a person asks of God." Only God knows better than this person what she or he needs most in the long run. When a person comes to prayer, God is already achieving the goal of creation, for in prayer a person is entering into a conscious love-relationship with God.

Yet petitionary prayer is not the high point of human prayer. Our deepest conversations, also, do not revolve around giving, receiving, and needing. Growing children occasionally speak with their parents about things other than getting help in their need; if not, their conversation remains infantile or adolescent. When prayer remains synonymous with "asking with insistence," the believer gets bogged down in a naïve and immature prayer-mode. Praying is not a magic button for getting supernatural interventions. Prayer is entry into relationship with God arising from the two-fold realization that, on the one hand, there are things that we ourselves cannot do, arrange, or rescue, and that, on the other, for those who love God, everything will ultimately work out for good. In other words, petitionary prayer arises from the accurate realization that we are limited, and that almighty God is good.

The most noble prayer-form is contained in the words, "Thy will be done!" These words are not uttered from a sort of defeatism or despair, but as a result of the insight that nothing better can happen to us than God's will and plan. The declaration that such a prayer must be superfluous because the will of the Almighty will prevail anyhow betrays a totally false image of God. God is a loving Father, not a blind tyrant who has always arranged everything in advance and independently. Not everything that happens is according to God's will. Far from it! For example, God does not will sin at all, and yet there is a lot of sin interwoven in daily events. God gave humans free will, even though he foresaw what its consequences would be, namely, the highest and lowest of what is possible on earth: personal love and massive destruction.

Even so, it is still not clear whether petitionary prayer for third parties really can benefit them. When a mother prays for her sick child, it is surely meaningful that, after years of a busy and harried life, she has this occasion to return to true prayer. But is the child itself thereby benefited? For it is first of all on account of her child that the mother is praying.

Mediation

If prayer for third parties were meaningless, the life of every Carmelite nun or Trappist monk would be no more than an egocentric flight from a despicable, dangerous world. But in reality, a good number of people in God's Church are called to intervene for others. People who pray are mediators or "go-betweens" for third parties.

The biblical notion of "mediator" has nothing to do with the familiar "social mediators" from our economic and political life. Such a social mediator is someone who is in some sense acceptable, or at least appears neutral, to both parties who are at odds (e.g., labor unions and management)—a sort of deft pilot that maneuvers the ship of politics between Scylla and Charybdis. But the biblical mediator is a good deal more than a supple diplomat. This is someone who is loved so much by God and who lives so intimately with God that God throws the mantle of mercy over all those for whom the pray-er prays.

Moses functioned in such a mediatory role for his people Israel: "Therefore He said He would destroy them—had not Moses, His chosen one, stood in the breach before Him, to turn away His wrath from destroying them" (Ps 106:23).

Abraham, too, goes up and prays for the corrupt and threatened cities of Sodom and Gomorrah: " 'Let not the Lord be angry, and I will speak again this once. Suppose ten [just] are found there'; and He [Yahweh] answered: 'For the sake of ten I will not destroy it' " (Gen 18:32). On account of Abraham's prayer and for the sake of ten people of prayer in these cities, God is willing to save the whole population and take them under divine protection, no matter what the sin and religious apathy of this folk may have been (and may still be).

Ruusbroec regards it as the first social task of a priest to pray for his congregation or parish: "For the priest reads his Mass, while the farmer sows his grain and the sailor sails the sea; and each of them thereby proffers his service to the others" (J. van Ruusbroec, *Werken*, vol. 2, 320).

Naturally, Christ is the mediator par excellence. In his historical life, he continually intervened between God and the people who had become alienated from God. Christ is the bridge between God and humanity. This is a task, moreover, that he is still carrying out since his resurrection, especially in the Eucharist. Each Eucharist is a new prayer of Christ (and of a small group of those belonging to him) to the Father, for the many who are absent, whether physically or spiritually.

Yet one should not imagine that the mediatory prayer of a handful of the devout is a sort of magical process by which results are extracted from a grim God who expects compensation and satisfaction. The most profound reason why prayer for third parties can be effective is best made clear by the mystics. We read in *The Temple of Our Soul*, a work by an anonymous author from the sixteenth century, that the mystic "himself was the heaven of the Holy Trinity: it was a delight for God to dwell within him and thus to be among the children of humans." In other words, the person of prayer (e.g., the mother for her child, Abraham for the Sodomites, or Christ for his enemies) is, as it were, a sort of tabernacle or "pied-à-terre" in which God is present in a special way here on earth, a place in which the ultimate end of creation is already realized in advance. Little by little, God is already becoming "all in all" by being partially experienced and addressed in some chosen persons.

The person of prayer (like the poor person) is a sort of spiritual bridgehead in which God's liberation can have a real beginning. In the person of prayer (as in the poor, hungry, naked, and emprisoned who are the "least of our brothers and sisters"), God is sacramentally present, accessible, and operative for all.

In all great religions the ultimate human destiny is the same: to be united forever with God. Now, in the person of prayer, something of this ultimate destiny is already present here on earth. "God comes everywhere that people let Him," wrote M. Buber. It is true that God is everywhere, and present in all humans. But God comes in an ever new way (and is experienced in an ever more insistent way) whenever a person consciously admits God. Concretely, this means: when a person begins to pray.

The family doctor can be called to the bedside of a sick person by a concerned member of the family or by a friend, even though the patient may not wholly see the necessity. Analogously, the "advent" or new coming of God can be hastened and realized by the prayer of one who leaps into the breach for a friend.

In what does the "operation" of God consist when he is called on for help? What does God "do" for a person when called on for help by a third party? We find the answer in Scripture, where it is said of Christ: "He went about doing good and healing all that were oppressed by the devil" (Acts 10:38). Another illustration is when he is asked by third parties such as in the case of the daughter of Jairus, the servant of the centurion, or the son of the widow of Naim. God comes to liberate us from every form of evil and suffering, even though we ourselves do not always know what is the most urgent of our sufferings.

Faith and Transformation

In addressing the lame man, Jesus first spoke of his sins, even though the man was not really brought to him for this. Only after that did bodily healing follow, as a symbol of all that went before. When third parties ask for a cure, God always heals in a way that, for the most part, transcends the human capacity for understanding. In essence, Lourdes is a religious, not a medical, center. This is why, in Lourdes, there are more miracles of a religious nature and conversions than medical cures.

Thanks to his own grief, Paul discovered that God is never closer to us than when we feel weak and helpless. As Paul tells us himself, three times he asked the Lord with great insistence to cure him of an illness that meant a grave handicap for his apostolate. Exegetes suppose a form of severe epilepsy, which in ancient times was considered possession by the devil. Thus, it was an illness that was bringing his apostolate and integrity into discredit. "Three times I sought the Lord about this, that it [Satan in my flesh] should leave me; but He said to me: My grace is sufficient for you, for my power is made perfect in weakness" (2 Cor 12:8-9). Hereafter, Paul would "boast of [his] weaknesses." Infirmities, poverty, and suffering are, as it were, "magnets" that attract God in a special way. The notion of his own infirmity and psychological misery had this positive result for Paul: God, and not his own personality, became the gravitational center of his preaching. Paul preferred not to speak much of himself, but all the more of Christ, because he thoroughly realized that his own appearance and "image" displayed weak traits. On account of his infirmities, Paul was no longer "self-confident" in the true meaning of the word. His only certitude came from his faith; that is to say, it was rooted in God.

When Paul treats of the meaning of prayer for others, he points to the "mystical body of Christ." In fact, he uses two images in order to illustrate the connectedness and necessary solidarity of people with each other. Believers together form "one body" or "one building, built upon the foundation of the apostles and prophets, Christ Jesus Himself being the cornerstone in whom the whole structure is joined together" (Eph 2:20-21). In a building, one stone supports the other, even though all stones are far from being equally central and important; not all stones have to bear the same weight; not all people have the same vocation. "For as in our body we have many members, and all the members do not have the same function, so we, though many, are one body in Christ, and individually members one of another" (Rom 12:4-5).

We are especially recommended to pray for one another. From those who have received the gift, and thus the vocation, of a more intimate or even contemplative prayer, a special help is expected for all who come up short in that respect or who seem to be immature. The word of Paul applies to persons of prayer or contemplation more than to all others: "None of us lives to himself alone" (Rom 14:7). In various ways, people can and must leap into the breach for each other. Most of all, if they are Christ's disciples, they must intercede with God for each other.

Therefore, the person of prayer is a mediator between the sufferer and the healing God. Through the suffering of those who have a special place in our hearts, God is calling us closer to himself.

The Egyptian monk John Climacus calls prayer "the mother and daughter of tears." Prayer is especially the "daughter," or the result, of tears because for many, suffering and pain form the first occasion for seeking the Lord's help. In this sense, the saying that there is never so much prayer as in times of war and want is right. Yet true prayer is much more than a life-buoy for stormy times.

In the case af the mystic, one can also call prayer "the mother" of tears, because "the gift of tears" (or being moved and seized unto tears) is not an unusual phenomenon in contemplative prayer.

The gospel repeatedly affirms that petitionary prayer is always effective: "Everyone who asks, receives; and he who seeks finds, and to him who knocks it will be opened" (Luke 11:10). It will be effective, on the condition that we pray with faith and confidence. At first sight, this last little clause seems to be a handy, not to say cunning, argument often used by pious preachers to explain why certain people's ardent prayer finally goes unheard: "perhaps he prayed with too little confidence," or "his faith was perhaps laced with hidden doubts."

But faith is not the same as being psychologically convinced of a happy outcome. And confidence in God is something quite different from "not for an instant doubting the result of my prayer." The opposite of the prayer of faith is not prayer which is part confidence, part doubt. The opposite of the prayer of faith is magical, mechanical practice.

Faith is not a question of reaching a psychological condition in which no more doubts exist. One can never definitively weed out the tares of doubt, even in the holiest little garden on earth. Rather, to have faith is to enter into relationship with Someone who we know is almighty and infinitely good. Faith is a spiritual bondedness, not a psychological attitude or intellectual certitude. In other words, faith is not a question of moods, but of relationship. This relationship never entirely excludes psychological doubt and human feelings of insecurity. People who by nature are anxious, pessimistic, and hesitant can also pray in faith and confidence. Meanwhile, on a purely psychological level they perhaps do feel more doubt and disquiet

than stable certitude. And yet their prayer can show a
pure quality of faith.

Isn't the fact that people pray already a proof that they
believe and trust? Is there really a prayer whose quality of
belief is so low in carat-value that it can scarcely be called
"gold," that is, faith-filled? This is indeed the case when
prayer is reduced to magic formulas, efficient practices, or
amazing techniques. In such cases, let us no longer speak
of faith but of superstition. The fact that a person mum-
bles certain formulas, uses Lourdes water, or puts St.
Anthony's statue in just the right spot has nothing to do
with prayer. In order for it to become prayer, this childish
attention has to be directed toward God and not to
methods considered miraculous.

Where there is true prayer, God is present and heals.
How the God of salvation will answer is no easier to pre-
dict than how a good doctor will ultimately react to the
complaint of a patient and then do something about the
pain. Good doctors know much better than their patients
what is good or necessary, or even dangerous, for them.
The important thing is that the patient go to the doctor,
trust him or her, and be willing to cooperate. Those who
pray are heard on account of the faith with which they address themselves to God, not because of their mental or
physical achievement (e.g., nine First Fridays, or walking
fifty miles to a Marian shrine). Yet the pray-er will often
react to the word of Christ, "Everything is possible for
those who believe," with the humble faith of the pos-
sessed young man: "I believe; help my unbelief!" (Mark
9:23-24). In the Gospels, every prayer is a human mixture
of faith and unbelief. In the Hebrew Scriptures, the unhappy Job in his long and stormy petitionary prayer suddenly says: "But he does not even listen to my cry,
though I know surely that He hears me" (cf. Job 9:16).
Only believers speak this way, believers who, on account
of their problematic suffering, remain tormented by
doubts. On the one hand, they know for sure that no
word of their prayer escapes God's loving attention. On
the other, they doubt whether God will be "obliging,"

that is, whether everything will go as they had dreamed and wanted it to. Only in their best moments do believers realize that nothing better can happen to them than God's will.

Even though the situation of need prompting those who pray to call for help does not always change, one thing definitely does change: the pray-ers themselves. More precisely, prayer does not change things or situations but it changes the people who must live in a painful context for the time being.

First and foremost, prayer heals the spirit and the love-orientation of those who pray. Yet people are not pure, abstract spirits. They live in a concrete historical situation. The whole gospel demonstrates that Christ was not a "soul doctor" concerned with nothing but spiritual needs, like a dentist who is confined to the care of oral infirmities. Christ had concern for all human needs, even for the most physical and material, even though he never regarded the latter as separate from the whole person. Matter, too, has to do with God. This is why prayer cannot be limited to "purely spiritual" matters. Christianity is not a "religion of pure spirit," as some Protestants often have incorrectly thought in their—understandable—dislike for devotional forms that were all too reified. The exterior and bodily reality is important and precious for Christ (and thus also for Christianity). Distrust of transitory and secular reality, so strongly characteristic of Eastern religions, is foreign to true Christianity. Because God is deeply concerned with the whole of human life, physical as well as spiritual matters can receive a meaningful place in our prayer.

Unfolding Our Deepest Need

In an essay on happiness, Simone Weil noted: "If there were no unhappiness in this world, then perhaps we would imagine we were already in paradise" (S. Weil, *La Pesanteur et la Grace*, 85). If suffering, failure, and death were excluded, if everything went smoothly, would life be more than a game without any urgency? According to this foolish hypothesis, would prayer be anything more than a luxury which we would be free to take or leave? Isn't the idea that our time is limited the main reason we take the things we are doing so seriously?

Suffering increases our spiritual capacities and seriousness, just as a feeling of panic often increases our physical capabilities. In time of need a person can withstand, dare, and accomplish more than in times of abundance and general well-being. Suffering not only relativizes many accidental things, but it forces us—if we want to keep our head above water—to call on our last spiritual reserves.

Because God dwells in the depths of our being, suffering almost always leads to a confrontation with God. In suffering, prayer becomes almost self-evident. Only when our happy game is interrupted does the question arise as to what is really important. Is it any wonder then that this suffering leaves its mark on our prayer? In a certain sense, every prayer originally has something of petitionary prayer about it. So it is not accidental that the etymology of the Germanic word *bidden* (pray, as in "bidding prayers") and of the Latin word *precari* first and foremost refers to asking, seeking, beseeching. Begging (in Dutch, *bedelen*) is the frequentative of *bidden;* the beggar (*bedelaar*) is someone who prays (*bidt*) with insistence and repetition.

Yet this beseeching and begging is not the highest form of prayer of which we are capable (and to which we are called). In truly mature, adult prayer, it is no longer God who hears us, but we who finally lend an ear to God. The pray-er, it is true, seeks constant contact with God, but God is ceaselessly waiting for a human response.

"Behold, I stand at the door and knock; if anyone hears my voice and opens the door, I will come in to him" (Rev 3:20), says the Lord in Scripture. True prayer exists as soon as we have heard God and opened the door of our heart to him. This "hearing" and "opening" can take place only when we become calm interiorly, that is, where we free ourselves of obligations, cares, plans, and intentions. In a word: when we cease "to beseech."

In perfect prayer, God does not overwhelm a person with supernatural words, thoughts, or enlightenment. Rather, God "touches" us and changes us in our manner-of-being. In those who pray, something is always "happening," even though this happening can scarcely be felt, and even though it is seldom what they had hoped or prayed for.

What actually happens in those who truly pray is that God takes over the helm. God's will can then be done without resistance. The most striking result of God's operation in pray-ers consists in the fact that the image of God they held up till then is retouched. Their vision of God changes. They notice that God is other than they had imagined. As Jesus himself put it, "I will . . . manifest myself to him" (John 14:21). For radically conservative people, this is always a great difficulty, because they like to cling closely to the image of God they bear within them and have revered since childhood.

That God is other than we had always imagined becomes especially clear in the prayer of those who suffer. Suffering, too, changes our self-made image of God, even in a shocking way. In the first stage, those who suffer most often begin to ask questions about God. In a certain sense, suffering is first a centrifugal or "God-fleeing" force. For a while, it seems to distance us from God, smashing to pieces our precious image of God. It undermines our trusted convictions. In a second stage, it appears only to have driven us away from self-made images of God which are outmoded and no longer tenable.

The love of God acts like every love worthy of the name. We gradually discover and accept that the partner is *other* than we perhaps had at first naively imagined and dreamed him to be. (Many people never get this far; this is why love and true faith are not all that self-evident.)

The "otherness" of God ultimately comes down to this: God seems to be much more real and near than we had previously imagined. Suffering sculpts and retouches an image of God which is continually being purified, while it throws a mantle of improbability over naive human religious fabrications. Rilke correctly writes:

> We build images of You like walls
> because a thousand walls already conceal you.

Suffering comes over us like a terrible storm-wind that blows down human screens and walls. This is how God finally becomes in a sense visible, even if it be in the nakedness of faith now purified.

Conclusion

We can best summarize the Christian view of suffering by comparing it to the outlook on suffering professed by other great philosophies of life, such as Hinduism, Buddhism, and Stoicism. For all Eastern religions, suffering is the primary foe. The basic goal of yogis, gurus, and Indian mystics is to find freedom and avoid suffering. For them, the fact that we suffer is the clearest proof that we are still bound to and in solidarity with the profane cosmos, history, and matter. We should detach ourselves from these things as soon as possible, for example, by asceticism, techniques of concentration, meditation exercises, or the exclusive contemplation of "metaphysical" reality, which is, after all, the only reality.

Other than this metaphysical reality, everything is only appearance and illusion. "The Indian rejects and depreciates *this* [earthly] life, because he knows that *another* Reality exists, which is apart from the process of becoming, history, and suffering" (M. Eliade, *Patanjali et le Yoga* [Paris, 1982] 15). For the Oriental, then, there are two worlds: a world of exteriority and appearances (in which suffering is unavoidable and endless) and the world of the "true self" (where all suffering is excluded).

Liberation from suffering is largely reduced to a refusal to pay any attention to the outer world (through asceticism and detachment), and as a consequence, to concentration on the timeless world of the true Self (through meditation and enlightenment). Human misery is not to be blamed on some kind of divine punishment or original sin, but on the imperfections and "illusions" of people who busy themselves with banalities. In other words, the cause of all suffering is the mixture of time and eternity, exteriority and interiority, or action and religious contemplation. For Christians, on the contrary, this mixture is central and essential. Christians reject every form of dualistic thinking and especially dualistic living. They fight against suffering through action (e.g., by scientific research, charitable institutions, development-projects, etc.) and they contemplate suffering (e.g., in the passion narrative of Christ, the poor, the handicapped, the exploited, etc.).

In Christian eyes, that which Orientals and Stoics call "detaching oneself from suffering" is, rather, a form of repression; we no longer want or try to consider a particular part of reality as mere illusion. That would be a form of alienation. The Oriental wants nothing to do with anything not belonging to "the true Self" (including, for example, suffering).

Moreover, Christians shudder at the somewhat exclusive term "self." For Christians, it is essential to surrender this individual "self" into the arms of the Other (i.e., the Beloved). Orientals try to free their "self" from the earthly world. Christians, however, find this terrestrial world holy. It is a gift of God and by no means an illusion. It is a "laboratory" or workshop in which eternity is prepared for by making the temporal realm more human or worthy of humanity. In other words, the earthly world is the matter or raw material used by the creative person to sketch or design projects that will have eternal value because they will be finished by God.

Oriental religious people and Christians alike take a position against suffering. The former try to ignore it; the latter, on the contrary, take the bull by the horns. This is a struggle in which they by no means stand alone. In the footsteps of Christ, they try "to go about doing good throughout the land." Whereas Orientals strive after redemption from the earthly—searching for their "true self"—Christians try to find redemption from being enclosed in their own self in going out to the Other.

Brahman yogis and fakirs preach renunciation of nature; but Christ preaches "*self*-renunciation." True, the two conceptions are not diametrically opposed; they even manifest remarkable and felicitous points of agreement. Nevertheless, we may not lightly overlook the important points of difference regarding the approach to and evaluation of suffering. We would do so at the risk of missing the core of Christianity, namely, the notion and the belief that the only way that offers an exit is the path leading from the Cross to the resurrection. For Christians, this Cross is certainly not an illusion or an object of minor importance. Rather, it is something holy and indispensable.

A last reflection ought to be added to this. In our considerations of the meaning and significance of suffering, we have perhaps created the impression that this suffering always, automatically, works toward the good. But nothing is less true. In human history, suffering has caused a great deal of irreparable destruction. It *always* does, even by nature. Only under well-defined conditions can and will suffering become fruitful. To put it more exactly: it is only under *one* condition that suffering receives the amazing power of a dying grain of wheat. This condition is that we see suffering in a context of faith and in religious perspective. "We know that in everything God works for good with those who love Him, who are called according to His purpose" (Rom 8:28).

The essence of Christ's message is contained in this "decree": not only Jews (as the Hebrew Scriptures originally thought) and not only "the predestined" (as the young Calvin thought) but *all* people are called—Jews as well as Greeks, sinners as well as saints, free people as well as slaves. All are "called," but they remain fundamentally free to respond to this message or not. The sufferer has the choice of many paths. All these paths, with one exception, end in destruction. This "exceptional way" is best epitomized in the life of Jesus Christ as this stands depicted in the Gospels and as it is experienced in Christian tradition. Our predecessors on this way are the countless saints and devout people who in the course of time trod this same path. Their lives are a witness to the "how" and "why" of this path.

Speaking of the famous adage of Juvenal, "Mens sana in corpore sano," G. Thibon writes, "A sound mind in a sound body is doubtless a nice thing. But the most heroic,

refined, noble, and vivacious thing in this world is a
sound mind in a sick body. That is, a mind that offers resistance to being contaminated by anxiety over this life,
and whose health is the fragile fruit of a victory."

Physical suffering and bodily decline are relativized by
Christ. They are not the ultimate evil. It is true they must
be combatted with all the means at our disposal, but
meanwhile they contain a positive and irreplaceable potential for spiritual deepening. It is only when it is set against
the background of the resurrection that the Cross receives
its true proportions: it is the only possible way to *salus,* a
true and lasting health. Psychological or mental pain also
takes on a different hue in the light of the Cross. "What
remains of our mental pains," says Thibon, "when we
successfully eliminate all the torments that come from our
ambitiousness, pride, lust, dreams, useless nostalgia for
the past, and empty anxiety for the future?" (G. Thibon,
L'Echelle de Jacob [Paris, 1975] 62, 69).

At the foot of the Cross, sufferers fighting for their
health and life come to the insight that at all times human
life rests in the hands of God. When we ultimately "yield
up our spirit," we are not giving our life back to "noth-
ingness"; rather, we lay this life in the hands of the One
who willed it, who created it, and who has providentially
guided it.

The mystery of suffering and evil remains a reality that
no one can "posit" or refute as a self-evident phenomenon. We have not tried to do this either. The whole history of Christian thought (and really, of all religious
thought) is a series of variations on this same basic theme.
In fact, the whole of Christian spirituality has kept itself
busy with this basic problem: how do we reconcile the
Creator's goodness with the evil within creation? How do
God's omnipotence and human freedom go together? How
can the biblical word, "and God saw that it was good,"
be brought into agreement with our modern sober view of
a world full of injustice, violence, and destruction? This
tension has kept Christian thought and Christian prayer
busy for centuries already. Even God's revelation does not

intend to offer a crystal-clear solution to it. It does bring orientation and light. But with the help of this light, we must all carve out our own creative course. Perhaps for the problem of suffering there simply is no single, comprehensive answer. Perhaps there are only various partial answers, and we are all called to construct our own, taking into account our own experience, our own suffering, as well as the precious insights of the many others who have ever wrestled with the problem (in other words, taking into account the whole treasury of Christian spirituality and the traditions of all great religions).

Many answers irritate us, not only because they seem too simplistic, but also because suffering cannot stand inflation of words and great theories. Perhaps we must listen especially to those who, in spite of their great grief, have nevertheless not lost their deepest peace. Even in the midst of their many questions, they have never forsaken the evidence of a growing faith in the goodness of God.